Uncle Arthur's
BEDTIME
STORIES
Volume Five

Painting by Robert L. Berran © by Review and Herald

Uncle Arthur's Bedtime **STORIES**

Volume Five/Arthur S. Maxwell

Published jointly by

REVIEW AND HERALD® PUBLISHING ASSOCIATION
Washington, DC 20039-0555
Hagerstown, MD 21740

PACIFIC PRESS PUBLISHING ASSOCIATION
Boise, ID 83707
Oshawa, Ontario, Canada

Contents

◄ Painting by Robert L. Berran © by Review and Herald

Lesson Index

Artists participating in the illustration of this volume are: Harry Anderson, Harry Baerg, F. W. Brouard, Fred Collins, Kreigh Collins, William Dolwick, Thomas Dunbebin, Jack Gourley, Arlo Greer, Russ Harlan, William Heaslip, William Hutchinson, Howard Larkin, Elfred Lee, Manning de V. Lee, Robert Mangus, Gerald McCann, John Steel, Harold Stitt, and Jack White. Cover by John Steel.

God's Little Workshop

THAT IS THE NAME George gave to the place where he did all his experiments—God's Little Workshop. What a good name for any boy's workroom or laboratory!

Here, working with God, he invented all sorts of wonderful things, searching out the secrets of nature with great patience and many prayers. From the humble peanut he made more than three hundred products, literally "from soup to nuts," including "milk," soap, soup, wood stains, axle grease, ice cream, and sugar!

From the sweet potato he produced starch, vinegar, ink, shoe polish, soap, paste, pickles, salad oil, wood stain, dyes of all sorts, and a hundred other useful things. From the common clays of Alabama he made beautiful and lasting paints.

Here too he studied how to fight plant diseases, how to grow better corn and cotton, and how to make farms and gardens produce much more than they ever had before.

Born in 1864, the year before the War between the States ended, George knew much sadness as a little boy. When he was but a baby, his father—a slave on the farm of Moses Carver, of Diamond Grove, Missouri—died from

◄ Photo by P. H. Polk. Tuskegee Institute.

Dr. George Washington Carver in his laboratory, which he called God's Little Workshop.

an accident. Shortly after, he and his mother were stolen
by bandits, the "night riders" of those old, bad days. George
was found and brought back to the Carver home, but his
mother was never seen again.

Mrs. Carver, "Aunt Susan," took the little orphaned black
boy into her home. He was small and sickly, and could not do
the jobs that other boys of his age were expected to do. So she
taught him sewing and knitting.

When he was still very young, George became interested
in flowers and plants. In the nearby woods he planted a little "secret garden," where he tried his first experiments
with growing things. He learned how to nurse dying plants
back to life, and he had such a magic way with them that
he came to be known as the little plant doctor.

He loved everything about nature. Sometimes he would
take a bunch of flowers to bed with him at night and fall

asleep with them in his hand. Sometimes, too, he would smuggle toads and frogs and creeping things into his bedroom.

Always he was asking the name of something he had found in the woods—every stone, insect, and flower that he saw.

While still very young, he went into a neighbor's house and saw a painting for the first time. He was greatly impressed. "Who did that?" he asked, and when he was told that a man made it, an artist, he said, "I want to do that someday." After that he was always drawing on boards and flat stones. He made colors for his paints out of berries, roots, and the bark of trees, then painted pictures on cans, pails, and bits of glass. This, too, he kept secret, like his secret garden in the woods.

How he wanted to go to school! But there was no school for black boys where he lived. The nearest was eight miles away, but he begged and begged the Carvers to let him go to it. At last, when he was ten years of age, they consented. The night he arrived at the school he slept in a barn, with rats running all around him. Then in the morning, as he sat on a pile of logs, hungry and lonely, a kindhearted lady, Mrs. Watkins, took pity on him and gave him breakfast.

12 After that she kept him in her home while he went to school. She taught him to pray and to love the Bible. When George was nearly eighty years of age, he was still reading that same Bible.

It was on his first day at school that George became George Carver—because he came from the Carver estate. Now he began to study hard. He loved it. He longed to learn. When the bell rang for recess, book in hand, he hopped over the fence that separated the school from Mrs. Watkins' house, and propped it up above the washtub so he could read as he scrubbed. When the bell rang again and recess was over, he dried his hands and hopped back over the fence to school. After school he did various chores for Mrs. Watkins, then read his books again. He was hungry to learn.

All his lessons, however, were not in school. He learned one caring for the lettuce. The geese had many baby goslings, eager to get through the fence to the lettuce, and George was supposed to keep them away. But George went off with the

boys and played marbles. When he returned, the lettuce patch was "as bare of greens as the palm of his hand." The goslings had taken the lot. He chased them to their muddy pond, but in his anger he overbalanced and fell in. George learned a lesson in trustworthiness that he remembered the rest of his life.

When he was thirteen he set out for Fort Scott, where he hoped to go to school. After a few weeks in school he would leave until he could earn enough for another term at school. Some boys would have given up, but not George.

To earn money he worked in people's homes—washing dishes, sawing wood, sweeping the yard. In the summer he worked on farms, and sometimes, when he was lucky, in somebody's greenhouse. Then he was really happy.

By and by he found himself in Minneapolis, Kansas. He worked in a home where he was taught washing and ironing. He learned so well that he borrowed money to set up his own laundry.

About this time he discovered that there was another

George Carver in town, a white man, who was getting his mail. So he decided to give himself an extra name. Thus he became George Washington Carver—a name that one day would be known around the world.

Little by little George added to his store of knowledge. At last he felt ready to go to college. So he applied to Highland University and was accepted. Happily he sold his little business and set off on his great adventure. Alas, when he arrived he was told that Highland University did not take black students!

George was crushed. This was the hardest blow he had had to endure so far. All joy went out of his life. He had only wanted to study and learn—why couldn't they let him do that? But no. He was shut out.

He tried farming in Kansas, but he had neither the strength nor the money to make a success of it. And all the time a great ache was in his heart. Alone, disappointed, and discouraged, he turned to animals for comfort. Soon every horse that passed was looking to him to feed it grass or sugar.

Those were dark days, but all the while he was learning things that would help him in God's Little Workshop.

Years passed by. George decided to go East again, perhaps to build a greenhouse and grow flowers or vegetables. He traveled while his money lasted, then stopped to work wherever he could find work.

Then one day in Iowa, ironing a shirt, he caught a new vision. He had been thinking, I know I can't, I know I can't, when something seemed to say, "You had better go back to school." "I can't," he said. "You can!" said the voice.

At this he dropped the iron, went to the open window, and looked out. At last he said aloud, "Well, then, I *will!*"

At this a great burden seemed to roll off his shoulders. Immediately he sold his few possessions and set out for Simpson College, hoping he would not be shut out there.

He was accepted and soon began to gain the attention of his teachers because of his bright, keen mind and his great desire to learn. The art teacher was amazed at the excellence of his paintings and did all she could to encourage him.

To pay his way, George opened up a little laundry again. He literally washed and ironed his way through college. It was a hard life, but he was happy. He was learning!

What would he do after he left college? How about agriculture—where his love for nature might be useful? He set out for Iowa State Agricultural College at Ames.

He arrived there penniless. In fact, he had nothing whatever but faith. So he went to work again, this time waiting on tables for the other students. But he was eating in the basement because he was black. Meanwhile he was learning! Now it was botany and chemistry—the great mysteries of nature he had always wanted to know. God was opening up His secrets to him! He was on the way to his workshop.

As he climbed the long flight of steps that led to the big red building where the agricultural classes were held, he felt that he was entering a new world. He was—a new world for himself and for thousands of others. Only God Himself knew that this was a great moment in history.

Four years later George was awarded a B.S., the first black graduate of Iowa State. A professor called him one of his most brilliant students and the sharpest observer of nature he had ever known. George deserved it all.

In 1896 Booker T. Washington, head of the Tuskegee Institute in Alabama, invited him to become a teacher in his school. Then began a friendship between two great men and a work known around the world.

All the knowledge of nature that George had won with such painstaking labor, he took with him to the South. But he had more to learn. Here were plants and flowers he had never seen before. Soon he began asking the boys at the institute, "What is this plant? and this?" Nobody knew. George decided that both he and the boys would find out.

The day came when there was not a plant or a flower or a seed or a bug that he could not identify. Once the students planned to play a joke on him. They showed him a bug made of the head of a large ant, the body of a beetle, the legs of a spider, the antennae of a moth, then asked its name.

He looked at it, then replied, "This is a humbug."

Another time three people on the Tuskegee campus decided that they would put George to the test to see whether he really knew the names of all the plants. So they brought along a large number of plants and a book that gave all their scientific names. Then they held up one plant, and George—now Dr. Carver, of course—gave the name. Slowly they turned the pages of the book to check it. Then they held up another plant, and he named that. Again they turned the pages of the book to see whether he was correct. After a while Dr. Carver got tired of it. Suddenly he picked up all the plants they had brought and rattled off their Latin names one after another so quickly that the three critics didn't have time to look them up. They were so amazed that they never doubted his knowledge after that.

Now he began his laboratory that he called God's Little Workshop. Here he brought all sorts of plants, soils, clays, and bugs, and studied them until he knew all about them. In this way he discovered the cause and cure of many plant diseases and how farmers could get larger and better crops from their land. Many times farmers would send him soil and ask him what was the matter with it. He would find out and then tell them just what to do to make it better.

Government people in Washington began to hear what was happening in God's Little Workshop. They sent men to find out. Sometimes they invited Dr. Carver to the Capitol. He began to write pamphlets with such titles as "Forty-three Ways to Save the Wild Plum Crop" and "One Hundred and Five Ways of Preparing the Peanut for Human Consumption."

Before he was through with the peanut he had provided the South with a yearly business of two hundred million dollars. Called to address a Congressional committee on the peanut, he was given ten minutes for his speech; but he took so many peanut products from the box he had with him that the Senators were astonished. He talked for an hour and forty minutes, and still they asked him to go on.

Edison, the famous inventor, heard of George Carver and offered him $50,000 a year to work for him. Many times Henry Ford offered him large sums to come to Dearborn, but he refused them all. He did not want money. He was satisfied to help people. A few years before his death he gave all the money he had saved to found the George Washington Carver museum. Here, today, you can see some of the wonderful things he did in God's Little Workshop; also, the tools he used there, such as a few broken bottles, a cup for a mortar, an inkwell with a wick stuffed in it for a Bunsen burner. With simple tools like these he made silk from the bark of poplar trees, rope from cornstalk fiber, paper from okra. Miracle after miracle came out

of that little workshop, all because a humble boy wanted to 19
feel he was working with God.

Then on January 5, 1943, all the world was saddened to learn that George Washington Carver had passed away. The little slave boy who worked so hard to go to school, then worked so hard with God in the little workshop, was resting at last. Because he worked not for himself but for others, his memory is cherished in every land.

And somehow I feel sure that God will be waiting for him with a greater and more beautiful workshop in that fair land, where all who love Him will explore the wonders of nature throughout eternity.

Policeman and the Pup

RALPH WAS SITTING on a bench in the park reading a book. On the other end of the bench sat two untidy and unwashed boys, talking happily together and occasionally throwing a pebble into the lake.

Suddenly one of them raised a cry of alarm.

"Look!" he cried. "There's a cop coming."

"Let's get out o' here," said the other.

A moment later the two were running away at top speed, while Ralph looked after them with interest, wondering what wrong they could have done and whether the policeman would run after them.

He did not. He may have seen them running, but showed no interest. He did not quicken his pace in the least. He walked by calmly on his regular round of the park, as if the two youngsters never existed.

By and by, after the policeman was well out of sight, the two boys returned and sat down exactly where they had been before.

Ralph's curiosity was aroused.

"Why did you run away when you saw that policeman

coming?" he asked with interest.

"We always do," said one of the boys. "Them guys don't care for guys like us. They'd lock you up in jail as good as look at you."

"Whoever told you that?" asked Ralph, smiling.

"The big boys at school said so," said the other boy, as though that settled the matter.

"But tell me," said Ralph, "have you done something wrong, that you are so afraid of a cop?"

"Aw, no," said the first boy, "we ain't done nothing wrong. We are just playing safe."

"I don't get it," said Ralph. "If you haven't done anything, why run away? If he's looking for a thief and sees you running he'll think you're guilty. And if you run when he tells you to stop you can get yourself shot. If you are O.K. you don't have to be afraid of cops."

"Aw, you don't know them," said the second boy, with an

air of wide experience. "If you knew 'em, you'd run away too."

"No, I wouldn't!" laughed Ralph. "There's no reason why I should run from policemen. They are O.K. most times. Look, here he comes again."

If Ralph had said, "Here comes a lion, or a boa constrictor," the effect could hardly have been worse.

The two youngsters looked around with terror on their faces.

"Let's get out of here!" they cried.

"No, don't," cried Ralph. "Stay. It will be all right. He won't bother you."

But off they went.

"Hide in those bushes over there," Ralph called after them, "and watch what happens."

To his surprise the boys turned quickly into the bushes and disappeared.

Some minutes later the policeman walked by.

As he passed the bench, Ralph stood up and, in his friendly way, said with a smile, "Fine day, officer."

"Yes," said the policeman, smiling back at Ralph. "It is a fine day. A very fine day. Enjoying yourself? I see you have a good book there."

"Yes, sir," said Ralph. "It's great." And he began talking about what was in it.

To the utter astonishment of the two boys peering through the bushes, the policeman sat down. And nothing happened to Ralph or the park bench or the bushes or themselves. The sun continued to shine in the sky and the ducks continued to swim on the lake.

After a few minutes the policeman rose, explained that he must continue his beat, and bade Ralph a friendly good-by.

When he had gone the bushes parted, and out came the two boys.

"But he didn't arrest you!" they said. "He didn't take you off to jail!"

"No, no, no!" laughed Ralph. "Of course not. He's not after me. He's after lawbreakers. Cops are just human. Treat them right and they'll treat you O.K."

I think Ralph was right. Policemen's work takes them among so many people who do wrong that they appreciate boys and girls who are courteous and respectful, kind and truthful.

A policeman can have a kind heart too. Some years ago in London I saw one hold back a long line of traffic while he took a poor old lady by the arm and helped her across the street. Not a car moved till the old lady was safe on the other side.

Look at the policeman shown on the next page. He was on traffic duty one wintry day in a New York suburb. His hands and feet were plenty cold as he stood there in several

inches of snow, guiding cars, trucks, and buses this way and that. Then, in the midst of the traffic, he spied a little pup.

It was in grave danger of being crushed by a car, and from the way it was running about, the policeman knew it was lost. No master or mistress stood on the sidewalk to call it to safety or take it home out of the biting cold.

The policeman was sorry for the pup and, holding back all traffic for a few moments, he picked it up.

But now what to do? He couldn't take it over to the sidewalk and leave it there because, for one thing, it would freeze to death, and, for another, it would probably run straight back to him, now that he had befriended it. And he couldn't give it to the first man or woman who passed by, because it was his duty to take all stray dogs to the police station.

What a fix to be in! And he had another hour on duty, too!

Then what do you suppose he did? The picture tells you. He tucked that little pup under his cape and held it there with one hand while he went on directing traffic with the other.

People going by in their cars must have said, "Look at that policeman with the pup!" No doubt boys and girls laughed and waved their hands.

And well they might have done. For it was a great thing for him to do. But, as I said before, policemen are always doing kind things like that. And if you keep the law and do right, they'll be your friends too.

◄ Photo by International

Tucking the pup under his cape, the policeman went on directing the traffic.

Just Too Late

WHY ELMER WAS always late getting home from school, I do not really know. He was just late, period. And when Mother asked him why, he couldn't tell.

Sometimes, of course, he had a good excuse. Perhaps his teacher had kept him in, or a bicycle tire had gone flat, or he had passed a car wreck and wanted to see it. When it was something like this, Mother usually said, "All right, dear. You couldn't help that, of course. But what keeps you late the other times?"

Elmer didn't know. Probably he just dawdled or stopped to talk to his friends. In any case the precious minutes were used up in one way or another, and Elmer arrived home half an hour, or even more, after the appointed time. Then he wondered why Mother wasn't pleased with him and why he had so short an evening to himself.

Mother talked to Elmer again and again about the importance of being punctual. She told him that if he didn't learn to be on time, he would have a weakness in his character that would plague him all his life. But she might as well have talked to a post for all the good it seemed to do

26

Elmer. Next day he would come home late again, with or without a good excuse.

Mother felt sure that it would take a shock of some sort to help Elmer learn his lesson. She was right. And it wasn't very long before it came.

One afternoon Father came home from the office in high spirits. Having finished his work early, he had suddenly thought of a bright idea to make his family happy, and, as usual, he wanted to carry it out immediately.

"Come on!" he cried. "Get your things on. Hurry!"

"What's all this about?" asked Mother, who was supposed to drop everything she was doing and enter into Father's plans at a moment's notice.

"I have the whole evening free," said Father, "and I'm taking you all to the sea. I've telephoned for reservations at the pier restaurant, and we have a table by the window right over the water. So come along now, come along! Let's not waste a minute!"

Very thrilled, Mother rushed upstairs to put her best things on and told Little Sister to do the same, and be quick about it. For the next few minutes there was much rushing and bustling in the house.

Then Mother remembered Elmer. Indeed, she couldn't help remembering him, for a voice downstairs was calling his name in loud tones.

"Elmer! Elmer! Where are you, Elmer?"

"I'm sorry," called Mother, "but he has not returned from school yet."

"Not back yet?" said Father. "Isn't he to be home at four?"

"Yes," said Mother. "But, er——"

"Four o'clock!" said Father. "That's about five minutes from now. I hope he's home on time. We can't wait for anybody. Not this afternoon. We must keep that appointment. Are you both nearly ready?"

"Yes, yes," panted Mother, out of breath. "We'll be ready in just a few minutes."

Mother hoped against hope that Elmer would arrive in time. But no Elmer appeared.

Father gave him fifteen minutes' grace, and Mother pleaded for another five. But at four twenty-five Father's patience gave out.

"I won't wait another second!" he said in a tone that Mother knew was final. "If the boy can't come home from school when he is supposed to, then he will have to learn his lesson."

And with that he released the emergency brake, put the car in gear, and guided it slowly onto the highway.

Half an hour later Elmer rode in on his bicycle. He went to the back door as usual, but found it locked. Then he tried the front door, but it was locked too.

"Funny!" he said. "I wonder what's up?"

He found the key and went indoors. On the kitchen table he saw a note that Mother had hurriedly scribbled before she left.

"We have gone to the seaside. Will be eating out on the pier. So sorry you weren't home in time. We waited nearly half an hour, just as long as we could.

"Love, Mother."

Elmer read the note two or three times. Then, as nobody was around, he threw himself on the sofa and burst into tears. To think that they had all gone to the seaside without him! Eating out on the pier, too! And Little Sister! That she should have this treat while he stayed at home was unbearable! If only he had gotten back from school on time!

That was a long, long evening for Elmer. It gave him plenty of time to think about his shortcomings. Again and again he thought of what Mother had said about wasting time and coming home late. He remembered how she had warned him that one day something would happen that would make him very sorry for himself.

Well, it had happened. But it wouldn't happen again. No sir! He had been late for the last time.

Overconfident Oliver

"OLIVER," CALLED MOTHER, "you won't forget to learn that piece you have to say at church, will you?"

"What piece?"

"You know, the one about the missionary who went to Africa and did so many wonderful things for the people there. Surely you remember. The young people's leader gave it to you last week."

"Oh, *that!*" said Oliver. "That's easy. I can learn that in no time."

"But you have only two weeks," replied Mother, "and I do want you to say it well."

"Two weeks!" snorted Oliver. "I don't need two weeks to learn that little piece. Two days will be ample."

"All right," said Mother, "but don't leave it too long."

A week later, Mother reminded Oliver again.

"How about that piece for Friday night?" she asked. "How is it coming along?"

"Oh, don't worry about that," said Oliver. "I still have plenty of time."

"I hope so," answered Mother.

So the days went by—the precious days when Oliver
might have learned his piece perfectly.

At last Thursday night came, the night before the meeting at which the piece was to be given.

"Don't you think it would be good to go over it together tonight?" suggested Mother.

"Go over what?"

"Your piece. You know. The piece you have to say tomorrow night."

"Oh, dear!" exclaimed Oliver. "I forgot all about it. You know, I have been so very busy all this week. But it won't take me long. By the way, where is it?"

Of course, it couldn't be found. That is, not until Mother and Oliver had almost turned the house upside down. At last Mother found it in the wastepaper basket, where it had been thrown by mistake.

Oliver looked it over quickly. "This won't be difficult," he said. "I'll have this all right by tomorrow night. Don't worry."

But Friday was a busy day too, and Oliver did not have as much time to give to learning his piece as he had ex-

32 pected. Nevertheless, he was quite confident it would "go over all right." Had he not "gotten through" similar jobs many times before—and with very little preparation? After all, he was only going to give it at the young people's meeting. There wouldn't be many people there, so what would it matter if he did make a mistake or two?

However, when Oliver arrived at church that night it was full. He had forgotten that this was to be a special night, some missionary anniversary. Of course, it had been announced, but he hadn't paid attention. Now as he glanced around at the packed church, he began to wish he had put more time on his piece. He wondered whether he really knew it well enough to say it at all. Then he began to feel hot and cold all over. There was a sinking feeling in his tummy. He wished he could leave the church and get away from it all.

But he couldn't. He was sitting on the front row. Several ministers were looking down at him from the platform. He was held there as in a jail.

Poor Oliver sweated it out through the first hymn, the prayer, the Bible reading, the second hymn, the chairman's remarks, the solo. Then at last he heard his own name called.

"We are glad," said the leader, "to have young Oliver here tonight. He is still very young, but he has given us many fine readings in times past, and we are happy and proud to have him with us again. Oliver!"

Oliver stepped forward and faced the audience.

What a sea of faces! He had never seen so many in the church before.

Then he began. As confidently as he could, he announced the title of his piece. Then he raced through the first few paragraphs. He could see some of the older people smiling up at him, as though saying, "What a dear boy! How well he can recite!"

Then, with awful suddenness, his mind went blank. It was as if he were riding along on his bicycle and the road before him suddenly dropped away, leaving a deep, dark chasm.

"The missionary," he said, "the missionary —— er —— the missionary —— er —— the missionary ——"

But he could not think what it was the missionary had done. If only someone would prompt him! He had intended to give the paper to Mother, in case he needed help, but he had been so sure of himself that he had failed to do so.

Now he was stuck, hopelessly stuck.

"The missionary —— er —— the missionary ——" he tried again.

But it was no use. He just couldn't remember. So, blushing to the roots of his hair, he stepped off the platform and hurried to his seat.

The minister, not quite sure what to say, coughed, and announced the next hymn.

"What a pity!" said Mother on the way home. "Just when there were so many people present."

"I know," muttered Oliver from the depths of his despair. "Don't say anything about it. Don't mention it. You were right."

It was a hard lesson for Oliver to learn. Very hard. But it was good for him. Never again did he leave the learning of a piece till the night before it was to be given. He took time, plenty of time, and learned it to perfection.

STORY **5**

Minimizing Milton

IF YOU ARE WONDERING what the long word *minimizing* means, let me tell you right away. It means making things seem smaller, "to reduce to the smallest possible," as the dictionary puts it.

And that's just what Milton did all the time. Not about the things *he* did, of course. These he magnified to the limit. But when it came to what his sister did, or what the other boys and girls at school did, why, he minimized them as much as he could. He seemed to hate giving credit to anybody except himself.

If another boy made a big hit at baseball, he would say, "Oh, well, it really wasn't much, you know; I've seen plenty of bigger hits than that." But if *he* made a big hit, why, he came home saying, "The ball would have gone clear over the grandstand—if there had been a grandstand there."

If a girl in his class got an A grade in some subject, he would say, "Just luck. I expect she'll get C's or D's in everything else. She's not much of a student, anyway." But if *he* got an A grade, why, you would think he had earned an M.A. or a Ph.D. by the fuss made about it. "Why, Dad," 35

he would say, "that was the hardest examination the teacher ever gave. In fact, they say it was the hardest ever given in the history of the school."

It was always the same. Magnifying what he did, minimizing what everybody else did.

One day Father picked up a drawing that was lying on the living room table. "Who drew this?" he asked. "Mighty fine job. We must have a budding artist in the family. Did you do it, Milton?"

"Aw, no. That was Sis. It's not too bad. But I guess she traced it."

"I did not!" cried Sis, coming in at that moment. "I drew it all by myself, Father."

"I'm sure you did," said Father. "And it's good, very good. Congratulations, dear. You must keep it up. One day you may become a famous artist."

"Sis, a famous artist!" scoffed Milton. "Ha, ha! That would be something. Sis with her little itsy-bitsy drawing book scribblings."

"Now look here, Milton," said Father. "I'm getting tired
of the way you minimize everything that everybody else
does."

"But I don't," said Milton.

"Oh, yes you do," said Father. "Just listen to yourself
for a few minutes and see whether I'm not right. Then listen to the Jones boy. He is always trying to say something
nice about other people. You never hear him say a thing
about himself."

"Aw, he's a sissy," said Milton. "He's no good at baseball or——"

"There you go again," said Father. "Just as I told you. I
cannot mention anybody's name to you but what you run
him down and find fault with what he does. As it happens,
the Jones boy isn't a sissy. He is a very fine lad, friendly
and helpful, and that means much more than being able to
knock a ball about."

Milton was silent. He was thinking. Could Father be
right? *Was* he always minimizing?

"Milton," said Father, "why not try magnifying for a
few days and see what happens? I don't mean magnifying
what *you* do, but magnifying what other people do. I think
everybody would like it a lot."

"Maybe he could begin on me," said Sis, with an impish
little smile. "I'd like it."

"That would be hard!" exclaimed Milton.

Yet it wasn't so hard as he had supposed. The next time
Sis drew a picture, and he was about to say all sorts of cutting things about it, he changed his mind.

"You know, Sis," he said, "there *is* something good about
your pictures. Really, I like them. You've got a gift, and no
mistake. Maybe Father's right—maybe you *will* be a great
artist someday."

Sis was so taken aback that she nearly slipped off her
chair. It was too much to take all at once.

"Milton!" she cried happily. "Did you mean that? Really? Why, that's the nicest thing you ever said to me!"

She jumped up and kissed him on the cheek.

Now it was Milton's turn to be surprised. "Aw, cut out the kissing!" he yelled, but he was secretly pleased that Sis cared that much about him. Then and there he decided to do a little more "magnifying." He would try it on Father and Mother, and the boys and girls at school. He did, and it worked.

By and by people began to say, "What a change has come over Milton! He has stopped bragging about himself and is always saying nice things about others. We like him."

Father's idea is a good one for every boy and girl to follow. Let's stop our minimizing and begin magnifying right away!

STORY **6**

Electric Eyes

AS A VERY SPECIAL treat Grandpa had taken Joanne to the city. They were going to make a day of it, seeing all the sights and eating in some very nice places.

As they came to the main entrance to the big new department store, Joanne put out her hand to push open the door, when suddenly it flew wide open on its own.

"Well!" she exclaimed. "Did you see that, Grandpa? However did the door open like that?"

"Like what?" said Grandpa, teasing. "You must have opened it yourself. There's nobody else about to do it."

"I didn't touch it!" cried Joanne. "You try it, Grandpa."

"Try it again," said Grandpa.

Joanne stepped out of the store, and the door closed behind her. Then she walked toward it again, and just as she put out her hand to push it, again it flew open by itself.

"I didn't touch it!" cried Joanne. "You try it, Grandpa."

"All right," said Grandpa, smiling. "I will."

So Grandpa tried it and, of course, the door flew open again.

"There's a mystery about this," declared Joanne, looking 39

all around the door, "and I'm going to find out about it.
There must be somebody watching inside this panel. Then, when a customer comes along, he pulls a handle."

"No, that's not it," said Grandpa. "But there is an eye watching there—not a human eye, but an electric eye."

"An electric eye!" exclaimed Joanne. "What sort of eye is that?"

"I'll try to explain," answered Grandpa. "But it's a bit difficult. You see, on one side of that door is an electric light that throws a narrow beam of light across the doorway onto a photoelectric cell on the other side. This completes an electric circuit, and the door remains closed. When someone passes in front of that light, the electric circuit is broken. Then various gadgets start working, and the door opens."

"How wonderful!" said Joanne. "But I still don't see how a beam of light could move a big, heavy door."

"You will learn about it when you take physics in high school," replied Grandpa. "But the electrical impulses, though very faint, are boosted up by transistors, like radio transistors, until they are strong enough to work a switch, which operates a magnet, which——"

"I see! I see!" interrupted Joanne, trying to look very wise. "And they call it an electric eye?"

"Yes, that's the name," agreed Grandpa, "because it sees everybody who comes through the door. Some jewelry stores have installed an electric eye to catch burglars. They say the crown jewels of England are protected by one."

"You know, Grandpa," said Joanne, "it reminds me of Mother."

"Does it?" asked Grandpa. "Why?"

"Because she sees everything, too," said Joanne with a mischievous smile. "I guess she must have electric eyes."

Grandpa laughed out loud. "You're right! That's just what she does have! She never missed anything when *she*

"There's a mystery about this," declared Joanne, looking around the door, "and I'm going to find out about it."

was a little girl. And I'll tell you something else, Joanne. That electric eye reminds me of God. He sees everything and everybody. And He sees much more than Mother sees. There is a text that says, 'The eyes of the Lord are in *every* place, keeping watch on the evil and the good' (Proverbs 15:3, R.S.V.). And there's another like it in Job, which says, 'His eyes are upon the ways of a man, and he sees all his steps' " (Job 34:21, R.S.V.).

"So God saw me going through the door, too!" said Joanne.

"Yes, and up the stairs, and—well—everywhere. There's no place on earth we can go, Joanne, but what the eyes of the Lord follow us. We are always in His sight. I remember another text which says, 'The eyes of the Lord run to and fro throughout the whole earth' (2 Chronicles 16:9, R.S.V.). That's a wonderful picture, isn't it? Moving eyes, looking everywhere. Seeing everything. Seeing everybody."

"I never thought of that," said Joanne. "It makes you feel that you want to be very careful where you go and what you do, doesn't it?"

"It does!" agreed Grandpa. "Mighty careful!"

"Guess He has electric eyes too," added Joanne.

"Something much more wonderful than that. In the first chapter of Revelation there is a description of Jesus, and it says, 'His eyes were like *a flame of fire*' " (Revelation 1:14, R.S.V.).

"That sounds like the beam of light by the door," said Joanne.

"Yes," said Grandpa, "but a thousand million times more powerful. For the eyes of Jesus not only see everything; they reach into people's hearts and start things happening and set great movements going. If we will but look at Jesus and catch the light from His eyes, there's no knowing what may happen to us."

"Now could we go to the toy department, Grandpa?"

"Of course, of course. We've hardly gotten through the door yet."

So off they went, but as they walked to the elevator, it was with a new sense of the nearness of God, and a new conviction that His eyes were following them all the way.

The Lighthouse Children

SOME YEARS AGO on a faraway, rocky shore stood a lighthouse. Night after night its brilliant beam shone out across the dark and dangerous waters.

Slowly the light turned, growing brighter, then fainter, then brighter again, never failing, ever warning of the rocks that lay beneath. Ships that passed in the night sailed in safety into the harbor. When their captains saw the light they knew that all was well.

Winter and summer the light blazed on. Through long, calm, starlit nights, through storm and tempest, it never went out. The deeper the darkness, the more brilliant it shone; the more terrible the tempest, the more welcome were its warning beams.

In that far-off, lonely lighthouse lived a man, his wife, and two children, Paul and Rene. It was a quiet and strange life for them. Their home was the tall, narrow lighthouse. Their life centered in the light above them. They were there for the one purpose of keeping the light burning.

One evening, as dusk was falling, Father climbed up the steep, narrow staircase, as he had done so many times

45

◀ Color Photo by T. P. Lake

Beside the tall lighthouse on a lonely rock by the sea lived a faithful lighthouse keeper with his brave wife and two children.

before, to kindle the light. In a few moments he returned, looking pale and sick.

"I am ill," he said, and collapsed in a chair.

Mother ran to him in deep distress, for it was clear he was seriously ill. For a moment all was confusion, and the children stood by, anxious and worried.

After a little while, when Father had been put to bed, Paul spoke.

"Mother," he said, "what about the light?"

"Go and see," she said. "I can't go now."

So Paul and Rene crept softly out of the little room and climbed up the cold, dark staircase.

Night had fallen. A storm was blowing up; dark clouds scudded across the pale moon. Below, great waves boomed on the rocks, the spray hissing as it curled back into the wild, raging sea.

The light was burning, but there was something wrong. Over the sea all was darkness, and the great beam from the lighthouse shone only toward the land.

"Rene!" cried Paul, "the shade is not turning. The ships will not see the light. What shall we do?"

"Can you start the machinery?" asked Rene.

"I'll try," said Paul.

Paul had seen his father do it many times and thought he could do it now. But he soon found that something seri-

ous was the matter; something had gone wrong. The machinery was broken, and he could not mend it.

"What shall we do?" cried Rene.

"There is the hand wheel," said Paul.

"But you could not turn that alone."

"No, but we could turn it together," said Paul. "Remember, Rene, we are the children of the light."

"I'll help you," cried Rene.

Seizing the great hand wheel, they began to turn it. The shade moved, and they were very glad. The ships would see the light after all.

Hour after hour they toiled on. No night had ever seemed so long. Their arms grew tired. Their hands became sore and blistered. Minutes seemed like hours, and hours were like days. They grew so weary that they wept as they turned. Outside the storm broke and raged in fury around them. Below, Father was very ill, and Mother was busy taking care of him. But still these children of the light kept turning, turning, turning the wheel. In utter weariness they carried on until a faint gray light in the east told them that their task was done.

Captains saw the light that night and thanked God for it. Yet they never knew what was happening in the lighthouse, or of the heroism of those two little children who were faithful to their trust.

Just as Paul and Rene kept the light burning through that long, stormy night, so God wants every child of His to keep the light of His love shining out into the dark, troubled world. The darker everything is around us, the more brightly our light should shine. The worse the storm, the more steady it should be. Nothing should be allowed to put it out. There are many people around us, like ships passing, who are looking for the guidance and friendliness that we can give them. So we who are children of the light must keep it burning through the night.

STORY **8**

Coals of Fire

"DADDY," CRIED DONOVAN, running in from school, "that Lionel is the meanest boy in the school."

"What's the matter with him?" asked Daddy.

"Oh, he's just terribly mean. He's always calling me names, and everything I do he says is bad or stupid, and he's always turning the other boys against me."

"It surely can't be as bad as that," said Daddy.

"Yes, it is," said Donovan. "And what's more, I'm not going to stand it any longer. Big as he is, I'm going to fight him tomorrow."

"Well, that's interesting," said Daddy, smiling. "I hope you will tell me when it's going to come off, so I can come along and pick up the pieces."

"There won't be any pieces left of him," said Donovan angrily.

"What? are you going to swallow him afterward?"

Donovan laughed.

"Do you know," said Daddy, "I can tell you how to pay that boy back."

"Can you?" cried Donovan, all eagerness. "How?"

"Would you like to put some coals of fire on his head?"

"Anything," said Donovan. "Anything."

"Well, I'll get the prescription for you so you can do it."

So Daddy went into his study and brought out a book. After a little searching he found the place.

"Ah, here it is," he said. "Listen, Donovan: 'If your enemy is hungry, feed him; if he is thirsty, give him drink; for by so doing you will heap burning coals upon his head'" (Romans 12:20, R.S.V.).

"Aw," said Donovan, "that's no good; I'd rather fight him."

"But," said Daddy, "this is much better. If you fight him you can't hurt him very much, but this way you pour coals of fire on his head. You will burn all the meanness out of him."

"Fine!" said Donovan. "But I don't like that way of doing it."

"Why not try it?" said Daddy. "It's worth trying, anyway."

"I'll see," said Donovan. "I'll think it over."

Donovan thought it over, and it was not long before something began to happen.

Next morning, on his way to school, whom should he meet but the hated Lionel.

"Just my luck," Lionel said as he came up with Donovan. "Got up late and missed my breakfast. Suppose you've had a big meal."

"No breakfast!" said Donovan kindly. "You must be starved. "Why don't you eat my lunch right now. Yes, I did have a good breakfast, and I am not a bit hungry, so here, have my lunch."

Lionel was as surprised as if he had received a blow between the eyes. He looked first at Donovan and then at the lunch.

"You don't mean it," he said.

"Yes, I do," said Donovan. "Here, take it."

"That's nice of you. Thanks," said Lionel, taking the lunch and beginning to eat. "But you'll have some yourself, won't you?"

Donovan took a sandwich, and they walked on to school together, munching in silence.

"Hot this morning," said Lionel after they had gone some distance. "Wish I could get a drink somewhere."

"A drink?" said Donovan. "Let me see, where can we get one? I'd like one too."

"Pity we can't get some lemonade in that store over there," said Lionel.

Donovan felt his pocket. "I have three dimes. What about it? Let's go over."

"Well, I don't want to take your money," said Lionel. "I'll wait till we get to the playground."

"Oh, no, come on," said Donovan. "We'll have a drink each. Looks good, doesn't it?"

So they went in, bought a bottle of lemonade each, and then hurried on to school.

That evening Daddy was waiting at the gate for Donovan.

"Well," he said, "how did the fight go? I hope you won."

"I did," said Donovan with a twinkle in his eye. "I just burned him all up."

"Whatever do you mean?" asked Daddy.

"Why, I did what you said. I fed him with my lunch, and I gave him a drink of lemonade, and—well, he suddenly changed. He's been different all day. We've been like old friends."

"Splendid! Well done, Donovan!" said Daddy. "I hope you'll win all your battles just like that."

STORY **9**

Today's Slaves

IT IS SURPRISING how many slaves are still to be found all over the world.

Once I talked with a man who held a very important office in the largest prison in the United States, and he told me some interesting stories.

His special work was to interview prisoners as they came in. He asked them about their homes, their families, their work, their education, and particularly what it was that led them to commit the crime that brought them into prison.

Do you know what most of these poor prisoners told him? Can you guess?

You should know.

Everybody should know.

They said, "It was drink, sir."

You know what that means? It means that before they broke the law they had been taking beer, wine, whisky, or some other alcoholic drink.

Oh, the sad tragedy of it all! In this prison there were more than 2,500 young men—their average age only twenty-four—who blamed drink for their fall.

52

Let us stand beside him for a few minutes.

Here comes a boy of fifteen—there are scores of them here as young as this. He has stolen somebody's car and has been arrested and sent to prison.

"Well, son," says this kind friend of the prisoners, "why are you here?"

"We began drinking, sir, and——"

The same old story.

Here comes a lad of eighteen. He has murdered an old woman, mistakenly expecting to find money in her house.

"Why did you do it?"

"Drink. Had a drop too much, I suppose, and didn't realize what I was doing."

Sometimes the prisoners are released on their promise to be good and lead a better life. All too many come back and have to face their kindly interviewer again.

"Why are you here again," he asks, "after having been given your liberty?"

"I went into a bar," is the reply. "I couldn't help it. And then——"

Another slave! Just one of thousands upon thousands, in bondage to drink.

None of us can take a wiser step than to promise before God that we will never, *never,* NEVER taste a drop of the evil stuff.

The only sure way to keep ourselves free from its clutches is never to begin.

Let's make the promise now—and keep it!

STORY **10**

Faithful
Unto Death

AS EDITH CAME IN from school, Mother saw at once that something was wrong.

"What is the matter, dear?" she asked. "You look as if all the troubles in the world were on your shoulders."

"Oh, Mother," cried Edith, "I'm tired of their teasing me, day in, and day out. It's always the same."

"What do they say to you?" asked Mother. "You mustn't mind a little teasing. Every little girl gets teased at school some time or other."

"Oh, it isn't just ordinary teasing," said Edith. "It's the way they keep calling me names, just because I keep the Sabbath. Why can't they leave me alone?"

Mother sat down and took Edith on her lap.

"Let me tell you a story," she said. "Then you will feel much happier about it. It's about three boys who were taken away into a foreign country and made to serve a king who didn't believe as they did. It was very hard for them. They wanted to remain loyal to God and His laws, but everyone around them was a heathen and a worshiper of idols. If they ever dared to speak of their religion, the people of the

54

land would laugh at them. Because they tried to be good,
the people would do all they could to annoy them and find
fault.

"Then one day they were brought to a very severe test.
The king got the idea that he would make a great golden idol.
He was quite proud of it and determined that all the princes
and rulers and leading men in his kingdom should bow
down to it. So he issued a decree that on a certain day these
people should gather on a great plain around the idol and
at a given signal fall down on their faces before it. To make
sure that everyone would obey him, he threatened that if
any should fail to bow down to it, he would have them cast
into a red-hot furnace.

"The three young men knew that the biggest test of
their lives had come. They could not avoid it, for they had
graduated from the king's special school and lived at the
king's court. So there they found themselves, in the midst
of a vast crowd of people, facing the great golden image that
stood in the center of the crowd. How their hearts must
have beat as they waited for the signal to be given! People
who knew them whispered together, wondering what they
would do now.

"At last the king's band began to play. There was a great
shout, and the huge crowd of people threw themselves face
down upon the ground. Over all that vast plain only three
figures remained erect. They could not have been more con-
spicuous. People began to look up at them out of the corners
of their eyes. The news spread rapidly from end to end of the
multitude. 'The three Hebrew boys have refused to bow down
to the king's image.' What excitement!

"There must have been a tremendous stir. Everybody
knew what the penalty was, and they waited to see what the
king would do. Meanwhile the three boys stood there, their
faces pale and set, bravely awaiting their fate.

"The king sent for them. He was in a bad temper. He

Painting by William Heaslip © by Review and Herald ▶

**The three young men successfully met the
greatest test of their lives because they had
learned to obey God and to trust fully in Him.**

asked them what they meant by disobeying his decree and warned them again of the fiery furnace. Respectfully, but firmly, the boys replied, 'Our God whom we serve is able to deliver us from the burning fiery furnace; and he will deliver us out of your hand, O king. But if not, be it known to you, O king, that we will not serve your gods or worship the golden image which you have set up' (Daniel 3:17, 18, R.S.V.).

"At this the king was still more furious and told his soldiers to heat the furnace seven times hotter than usual. Then the three boys were bound and cast into the furnace. That must have been a terrible moment for them. But they did not waver, not even when they felt the fierce heat of the fire upon them.

"Then a wonderful thing happened. The fire burned the ropes that bound them, but they themselves were untouched. Suddenly Jesus Himself appeared with them in the midst of the fire. The king saw the four figures walking there and was terrified. He called to the boys to come out of the furnace, and triumphantly they strode forth. The Bible says 'the hair of their heads was not singed, their mantles were not harmed, and no smell of fire had come upon them' (verse 27, R.S.V.).

"The whole concourse of people witnessed the miracle and must have been greatly impressed. As for the king, he admitted that the God whom the boys served was greater than his image. 'There is no other god who is able to deliver in this way,' he said (verse 29, R.S.V.). And so, because those boys were faithful and were not afraid to suffer even death for what they believed, the whole nation was blessed, and even the king was led to see the folly of his idolatry."

"I think I can see what you mean," said Edith.

"I'm sure you can," said Mother. "You are God's little witness to His truth at your school. You must be loyal to Him at all costs. You know that the Sabbath is right and

that God in His Word commands us to keep the seventh day holy. The others may tease you about it, but that doesn't matter. If you are loyal to Him in spite of all the unkind things they say and do, Jesus will walk with you at school as He did with the boys in the fiery furnace long ago."

"I think I feel better about it now," said Edith. "I'll try to be as brave as those three boys."

11

When Jack
Was Tired

MOTHER WAS SICK! Oh dear, what a difference it did make! For a time everything was in a great muddle.

Poor Daddy, finding himself responsible for the hundred and one jobs that Mother used to do, was nearly frantic, until at last in desperation he came up with a bright idea.

"Look here," he said to the children one evening, "the only way is for each of us to take a definite job and do it. If we all do our bit, we'll be able to manage till Mother gets better."

"But we have to go to school," broke in Jack, "and we have lots of homework."

"I know," said Daddy, "and it will mean your getting up a little earlier in the morning, but it will be good for you. After all, if you can learn to do these home duties now, it will make you better men and women when you grow up."

The children didn't think so at the moment, but they wanted to do what they could to help poor Mother. So they agreed to the plan.

Jack's job was to feed and water the chickens every

morning, and the twins, Tod and Tony, were to attend to
them every evening. Their morning job was to set the table
for breakfast and generally tidy up. Mary's task was to prepare Mother's breakfast and make the beds, and in the evening, to wash the supper dishes.

For some days the plan worked successfully and was a
wonderful help. Each child took real pride in his job and
tried to do it as well and as quickly as possible.

In fact, they were quite jealous of their jobs, at first.
When it was Tod's turn to bring in the coal, he made a
great fuss if Tony thought he would do it instead.

But as the days went by, the first zeal for the plan began to cool off. The pressure of schoolwork began to get
heavier, and the mornings began to get darker and colder.
It takes real grit to go down through the garden every
morning, wet or dry, hot or cold, to feed chickens.

One evening Jack came home late from school. He had
had a very busy day and was tired out. In addition he had a
great deal of homework to do, and the prospect of it made
him very cross. He was cross with Tod, cross with Tony,
cross with Mary, and, at last, cross with Daddy, which led
to his disappearance upstairs to bed. Daddy said he needed
sleep!

Morning came. The ringing of the alarm clock brought Jack out of bed with a jump. Half past six! Only an hour and a half before he must leave for school, and his homework still to do and the chickens to feed. How could he ever do it all? If only he had not been so cross with his brothers the night before! Then they might have helped him with his work, but now he dared not ask them. He felt too ashamed of himself.

He washed and dressed faster than he had ever done before and dashed downstairs to find his books still spread out on the table where he had left them. All his arithmetic and English still to do! Oh dear! And all the time he seemed to hear someone saying, "Chickens—you mustn't fail Mother; she's depending on you."

Looking at the clock, he decided to do the homework first and dash down to the chicken house afterward, though he did not see how he could possibly get through it all in time. Certainly he would not be able to help get any breakfast, and there would not be time for him to make up his lunch. But the math and English must be done. He plunged into them.

Meanwhile a conversation was going on between two
other little boys upstairs.

"Jack'll be late today for sure, and he'll be kept in
again." It was Tod speaking.

"Poor Jack, he'll never get any breakfast," said Tony
sympathetically.

"And I'm sure he won't have time to put up his lunch,"
said Tod, "so he'll starve."

"What about the chickens?" asked Tony.

"Yes, what about them?" said Tod.

"Shall we give him a surprise?" suggested Tony.

"He doesn't deserve it," said Tod; "he was awfully cross
with us last night."

"Yes, but then he was so tired, wasn't he?" replied Tony.
"And he is so nice to us sometimes."

"Sometimes," agreed Tod.

"All right then; let's slip out
the back door," said Tony. "Very
quietly now."

And with that the two little
figures glided noiselessly downstairs, quietly put on their garden shoes, and vanished into the
morning mist.

Half an hour passed. Three quarters.

Jack looked up at the clock. A quarter to eight! Only fifteen minutes before he must leave for school, and the chickens not done, and no breakfast.

He was almost ready to cry from sheer desperation.

Just then there was a loud bang on the back door. Curiosity led him to run and open it.

Outside stood Tod and Tony.

"Hi! Where have you two been at this time of the morning?" Jack cried in surprise.

"We've been feeding the chickens," said the twins, beaming all over, "so now you can have your breakfast."

"Feeding the chickens!" said Jack, swallowing hard. "I don't deserve it. Really I don't. I'm sorry. I'll bring you some candy tonight, I sure will."

"Goody!" cried Tod and Tony, running to warm their hands by the fire.

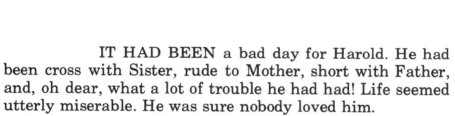

12

The Hurt in His Heart

IT HAD BEEN a bad day for Harold. He had been cross with Sister, rude to Mother, short with Father, and, oh dear, what a lot of trouble he had had! Life seemed utterly miserable. He was sure nobody loved him.

It was a very sad and lonely Harold who went to bed that night. He didn't mean to upset people so. He wanted to be good, but somehow he couldn't. Just when he made up his mind never to say anything unkind again, why, that was the very moment he said the worst thing possible.

He tried to say his prayers, but it was difficult. He kept thinking of all the naughty things he had said and done that day, and what God must think of him. Finally he gave it up, jumped up off his knees, and climbed into bed. But he could not sleep. His thoughts seemed to keep going round and round. What was the use of trying to be good when you couldn't be good? Why does a boy have to get into so much trouble and have everybody cross with him all the time?

Just as he began to despair he seemed to hear a little voice saying, "Jesus loves you; He will help you to be good." This was comforting, but how could Jesus make him good?   65

An hour or so later Mother went upstairs to bed. As she passed Harold's room she thought she heard someone crying. She stood still and listened. Yes, someone *was* crying. She crept softly to the door and looked in.

"What is it, dear?" she asked. "Are you in pain?"

"Oh, Mother, my heart hurts," he said.

Mother was at his side in a moment, wiping his tears.

"Whereabouts?" she asked anxiously. "Did you hurt yourself today? Shall I send for the doctor?"

"No, no, Mother, not that. I haven't hurt myself that way. It's just that I am sorry I have been such a bad boy. I want to be good. I want to do what Jesus wants me to do."

Mother dropped on her knees beside him. She knew that Jesus was speaking to him. This was perhaps the great moment for which she had been praying so long—the great moment when he would fully give his heart to God.

"All you have to do," she whispered gently, "is to tell Jesus that you love Him, that you want to be His child, and that you accept Him as your Saviour. Do you want to tell Him that, really, truly?"

"Yes, Mother, I do."

Then Harold got out of bed, knelt beside Mother, and told Jesus of the hurt in his heart and how he wanted to

give his heart to Him for always and always.

Just then Father came in. Seeing what was happening, he knelt down beside Mother and Harold. A moment later Big Brother and Big Sister came in and they too knelt. Then they all prayed for Harold, one after the other. It was a wonderful prayer meeting, one that Harold never forgot.

That night a boy was "born again"—born into the kingdom of God. And from that moment there was a great change in Harold. He was a new boy, a different boy. He was, as the Bible says so beautifully, "in Christ . . . a new creature."

As soon as they all rose from their knees, he was different. He wanted to talk about Jesus at once.

"You know, Mother," he said, "the devil was pulling me one way, but Jesus pulled me back. I am so glad."

Next day it was like sunshine after rain. Harold was radiant with his new-found love for Jesus. He was no longer cross and grumpy and ornery. Instead, he was kind, gracious, gentle, and respectful, a joy to have around the house. Instead of objecting to everything that Mother and Father suggested for him to do, he replied, "Of course, I shall be glad to help you any way I can." Instead of fighting with Big Brother and Big Sister all the time, he showed them such courtesy that they were amazed. "Why," they exclaimed, "something has happened to Harold!"

Something *had* happened to him. He had found God. He had given himself to Jesus. The Great Physician had healed the hurt in his heart.

13

Coal in a Cadillac

HOW OLD should a boy be before he begins to be polite? Ten would you say? Or nine, eight, seven, six, five, or four?

Fortunately for Dick, he learned to be polite when he was very young. From the moment he was able to talk, Mother taught him to say "Please" and "Thank you" and "Excuse me" and "I'm sorry" and "You're welcome" and other such words that help so much to make life pleasant for others and ourselves.

One day when Dick was not quite five years old he got on a bus with Mother. He was ahead, with Mother following, as they walked down the aisle looking for a seat.

Suddenly, as the bus began to move, Dick stumbled and stepped on a man's foot. The man yanked his foot away and looked upset.

"I beg your pardon, sir," said Dick. "I'm very sorry; I didn't mean to do it."

The man smiled. So did all the other passengers. Everybody was surprised—and pleased—to hear a little boy speak so courteously.

69

◀ Painting by Robert Berran © by Review and Herald

Suddenly, as the bus began to move, Dick stumbled and stepped on a man's foot. "I beg your pardon, sir," said Dick. "I'm very sorry."

Taking Dick on his lap, the man began to ask him questions.

"What's your name?"

"Dick Gentry, sir."

"How old are you?"

"Four, sir; but I'll soon be five."

"When's your birthday?"

Dick told him.

"Where do you live?"

Dick gave the man his address.

Meanwhile all the people on the bus were watching and listening. There was a smile on every face because one little boy was so good-natured, so friendly, and so very polite.

A few weeks passed. Dick became five years old. On his birthday, to his great surprise, he received a package. Inside was a note saying, "From your friend on the bus." But there was no name or address, so Dick couldn't write and thank the sender.

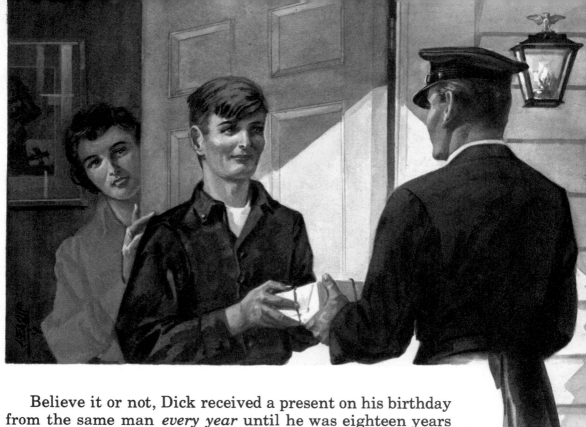

Believe it or not, Dick received a present on his birthday from the same man *every year* until he was eighteen years of age.

When Dick graduated from high school he received a camera worth $75, bearing the same words, "From your friend on the bus."

All this time he had no idea who his "friend on the bus" could be. Dimly he remembered sitting on a man's knee in a bus when he was a very little boy, but who the man was, he had no idea.

Then came a very cold winter. Coal supplies ran out. Coal trucks stopped running because there was no coal to deliver.

Dick was worried. His home was like an icebox. There was no coal for the fires. Father and Mother were not well, and they were feeling the cold severely.

Dick telephoned the coal company.

"This is serious," he said. "We're freezing. Could you please send us some coal?"

"Sorry," said the man at the coal company's office. "There's so little coal left that we're not sending out our trucks again till Monday morning."

"Till Monday morning!" gasped Dick. "I don't think my parents could stand the cold that long. I really would appreciate it if you could do something for us before then."

"I'm sorry," said the man. "By the way, what is your name?"

"My name's Dick—Dick Gentry, sir. Please help us if you can."

"I'll see what I can do," said the man.

An hour or so later a beautiful Cadillac stopped at Dick's house. A chauffeur stepped out and approached the door. Dick went out to see what he wanted.

"Is this where Dick Gentry lives?" he asked.

"Yes," said Dick. "Is there something I can do for you?"

"No," said the chauffeur. "I've brought you something."

Painting By William Heaslip

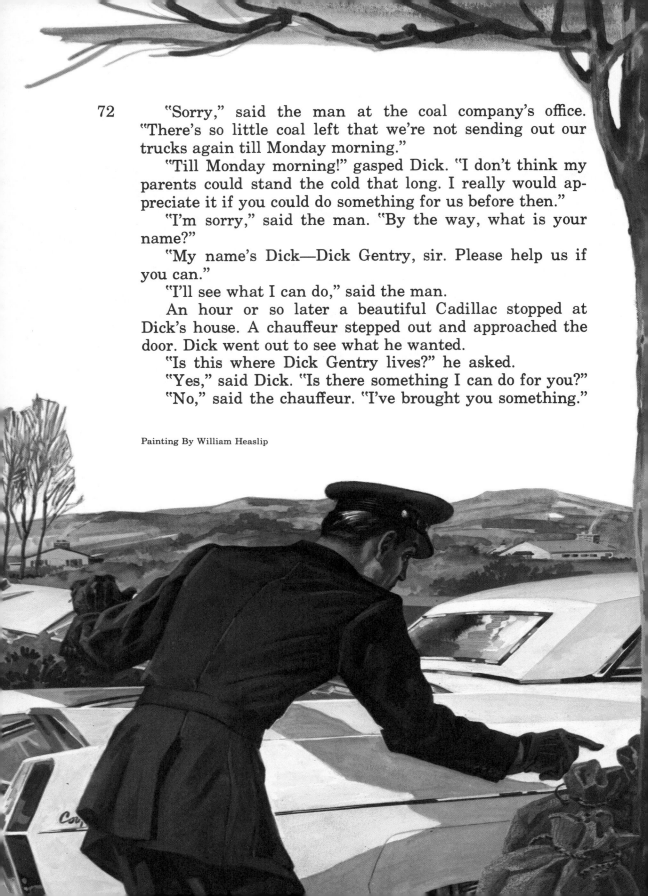

To Dick's astonishment the chauffeur hauled six sacks 73
of coal out of that beautiful Cadillac!

"Are these for us?" asked Dick.

"Yes," said the chauffeur. "And my employer says there's
no charge."

"Oh, thank you!" cried Dick. "Thank you very, very
much! But who sent them?"

"There's a note in one of the sacks," said the chauffeur,
and he said good-by and drove away.

Dick tore open the sacks. Inside one of them he found a
note. It read, "From your friend on the bus."

He could hardly believe his eyes. Then he guessed. The
man on the bus must be the president of the coal company!

Dick was right.

And all these kindnesses had come because a little boy
had been polite years and years before.

14

David's Daffodils

"HOW MUCH IS that pot of daffodils in the window?" asked David.

"Seventy cents," said the lady behind the counter. "And cheap at that."

"Phew!" whistled David. "What a lot of money! I'm afraid I can't buy it today."

"What do you want it for?" asked the lady.

"Oh, never mind," said David. "I'll be back."

Seventy cents! he thought as he walked down the street. Wherever would he get so much money!

He wanted that pot of daffodils so much! You see, every week he went to a Christian mission, and one day he heard a speaker say, "If you love God you will love other people. You are saved to serve. And if you can't do big things to help them, do little things. Take some flowers to a shut-in if you can't do anything else."

That's when the idea came to him. He would show his love for God by taking some flowers to Mrs. Gordon, the old lady on the floor above where he lived. Now he couldn't do it.

75

◀ Painting by William Heaslip ⓒ by Review and Herald

David got the idea that he would show his love for God by taking some flowers to old Mrs. Gordon who lived on the floor above.

Quietly he asked God to help him. Then he thought of
something. He would stop at a nearby furniture factory and
ask for some scraps of wood. Then he would chop them up
for kindling and sell them.

Pretty soon he was chopping away. He sold four bundles
to one person, three to another, and two to another. In just
a little while he had forty-five cents. But by now all the
wood was gone, and he didn't like to ask for more so soon.

Well, maybe the lady in the shop would let him have the
daffodils for forty-five cents.

"So you're back again!" she said as he walked in. "The
daffodils are still here."

"So I see," said David. "Er—well—er——"

"Well, what is it, boy?"

"Well, could you let me have the pot of daffodils for
forty-five cents? That's all the money I have."

"I'm sorry," she said. "The price is seventy cents."

David's face fell and he turned to leave.

"Just a minute," said a customer who had noticed Da-

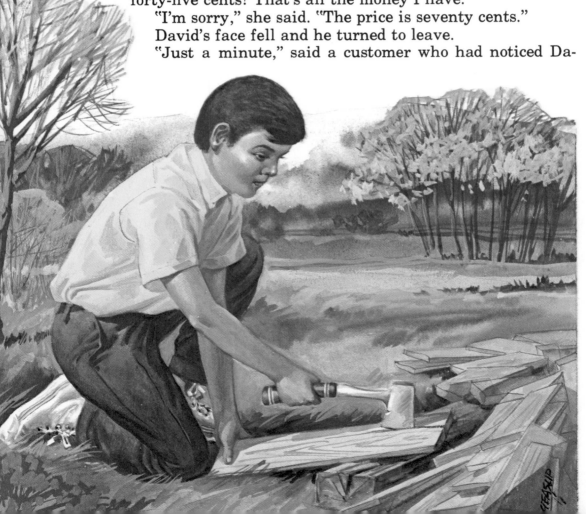

vid's disappointment. "Let me give you a quarter."

"Oh, thank you, sir," said David, "but I shouldn't take it from you."

"That's all right, son," said the man. "But why do you want that pot of flowers so much? Is it your mother's birthday?"

"Oh, no, sir. I want them for an old lady who lives in the apartment above us. You see, sir, she never gets any flowers."

"Is she related to you?"

"Oh, no, sir."

"Well of all things!" said the man. "Then why do you want to give them to her?"

"Because I love God and want to make other people happy."

The man turned away, his eyes filling with tears. David paid for the pot of daffodils, thanked his good friend, and

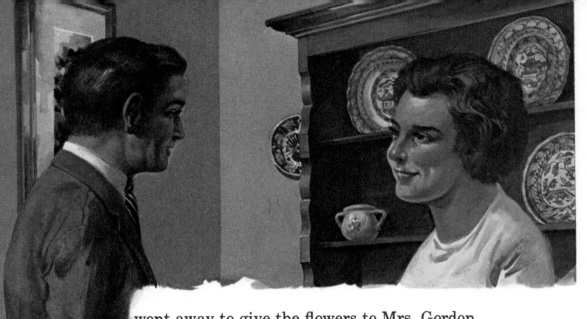

went away to give the flowers to Mrs. Gordon.

That night when the man arrived home he told his wife what had happened in the flower shop.

"I met the strangest little boy today," he said. "He couldn't have been more than nine years old. He was trying to buy a pot of daffodils for some poor old lady who wasn't even related to him. He didn't have enough money, so I gave him a quarter to help him out."

"I'm glad you did," said his wife. "But why was he doing it?"

"That's the funny thing," said the man. "He said it was because he loved God and wanted to make other people happy."

"I've never heard of such a thing!"

"I know. And it's more than we do. We say we love God, but we never give anything away or try to make other people happy. That is, outside the family."

"You're right. Maybe we should."

The man turned to his newspaper, but only for a moment. Suddenly he jumped up.

"Why don't *we* give some daffodils to people?" he demanded.

"Why not?" asked his wife.

"Let's take them to the mission tomorrow and suggest they give them to some of their old people who don't get any flowers."

"Let's," said his wife.

And so they did. Next day they turned up at the mission with a dozen pots of daffodils.

Just then they spotted David talking to the superintendent. "Why, that's my little boy!" said the man. "That's the one who gave me the idea!"

David looked at his friend, then at all the daffodils. His eyes opened wide, and a lovely smile spread over his face.

"What a lot of people you're going to make happy!" he said.

"Yes," said the man, "thanks to you."

STORY **15**

The Story of Trains

HOW EASY AND CONVENIENT it is for us to travel about nowadays! We can go almost anywhere by car, train, or plane. In this way we are much better off than the people who lived a hundred and fifty years ago, when a horse or stagecoach was the quickest way to get around.

Today, flying is so quick and driving so convenient that many children have never ridden on a train.

Nobody had ever seen a train or a locomotive before the War of 1812. Indeed, nobody knew how to make a steam engine. A man by the name of George Stephenson had the idea in his mind and was trying to work it out.

In 1814, at the age of thirty-three, Stephenson made his

first engine. He called it the *Blucher*. It hauled a train of eight loaded cars, weighing thirty tons, at four miles an hour.

Every year after that saw improvements and an increase in power and speed. In 1825 a railway line was laid between Stockton and Darlington in England, and though at first the managers thought they would have the coaches pulled by horses, Stephenson persuaded them to use his locomotives. The first train on this railway was composed of thirty-eight cars, weighing in all ninety tons. It started off at about twelve miles an hour, and even reached sixteen miles an hour, which was a terrific speed in those days. Indeed, people were so scared that a signalman on horseback rode ahead to make sure that no one would get run over!

Three weeks after this line was opened, a regular daily passenger service was started. Each passenger was allowed to carry only fourteen pounds of baggage.

Four years later, in 1829, the directors of the Liverpool and Manchester Railway, whose line was at that time under construction, offered a prize of $2,500 for the best locomotive. There were three entries, Stephenson's *Rocket* and two others. The latter two broke down during the trials, but the *Rocket* drew a train weighing thirteen tons, thirty-five miles in forty-eight minutes, an average speed of nearly

Courtesy, Baltimore & Ohio Railroad   Painting By Harold Stitt

Early contests won by the steam engine against horse-drawn vehicles marked an advance in transportation.

forty-four miles an hour. Up to that time, this was the fastest that man had ever traveled. People were more excited over this than we are when we hear of an astronaut traveling through space at 18,000 miles an hour.

So successful was this Liverpool-Manchester line that numerous other railways followed in England, and also in the United States (1830), Europe, and Canada (1835). Africa's first railway (1854) was in Egypt; Asia's (1853) in India; Australia's first in 1854.

Railroads became the life lines of great nations. Huge steam engines with driving wheels taller than a man, and later sleek diesels, crossed continents pulling mile-long freight trains or chains of streamlined passenger cars.

Nowadays there are some very long railways. The Canadian Pacific, for instance, runs 2,900 miles across the Amer-

ican continent, but the longest in the world is the Trans-
Siberian Railway from Leningrad to Vladivostok, nearly
5,500 miles.

So much for the trains that run on the surface of the
earth. How about those that run underground?

In 1863 the world's first subway line began operation in
London. Its first tunnel was dug as a trench, then covered.
In 1868 a "tube" line was added, built by a new method:
cutting a circular hole underground, more than ten feet in
diameter. In this method a metal shield is used, which
holds up the earth during excavation, gives room for building the permanent walls, and is pushed forward as the digging proceeds.

Many other subways have since been constructed, and
the foundations of many great cities are now honeycombed
with underground railways. New York, Chicago, and Phila-
delphia have them. Some of the companies at first used
steam engines to pull the trains, but soon, to avoid steam
and smoke underground, all these lines switched to elec-
tricity.

We have become so used to railways above ground and

below ground that we don't think of what it takes to build them, or of the great convenience they are to us. But, really, when you think of it, it is wonderful that we are able to travel so easily and rapidly. Just think how surprised the Bible prophet Daniel would be if he could wake up today. Wouldn't he just rub his eyes? Picture him riding on a superspeed train, or going down a moving stairway in Lower Manhattan, entering a subway train, and in a few moments coming up in Jersey City, on the other side of the Hudson River!

Long ago Daniel wrote that in the last days "many shall run to and fro, and knowledge shall increase" (Daniel 12:4, R.S.V.). People often apply his words to modern fast transportation.

Harry Baerg, Artist

And that makes me think of Isaiah, another prophet, who foretold the birth of Jesus and spoke about getting ready for His coming. He told the people to "prepare the way of the Lord" as if they were building a roadbed: "Every valley shall be lifted up, and every mountain and hill be made low; the uneven ground shall become level, and the rough places a plain" (Isaiah 40:3, 4, R.S.V.).

Wouldn't Isaiah enjoy traveling over the great iron roads for thousands of miles, across valleys and through mountains, on a straight, smooth surface! Don't you think he would be happy if someone were to tell him that millions of copies of the Bible have been carried on these railways (and on highways, too) to the very ends of the earth to make known "the glory of the Lord" (verse 5, R.S.V.)?

Truly this is the most wonderful time in all the history of the world.

The Little Girl Who Went to Sleep

JESUS LOVES TO BE KIND to children. They are all very dear to Him.

Once there was a little girl just 12 years old who was very sick.

Her father's name was Jairus—Mr. Jairus we would call him nowadays—and he was a leading man in the local church. In those days they called him a "ruler of the synagogue."

Now, Jairus had great respect for Jesus and believed that He was able to heal the sick. So as soon as his little daughter became seriously ill he ran to where Jesus was talking with the people and asked Him to come as quickly as He could to make her better. Jesus agreed to go.

Meanwhile Mrs. Jairus watched beside the little girl's bed and saw her growing weaker and weaker. There was nothing she could do for her that had not been done already. Would Jesus come in time? Why was He so long coming? What had happened?

An hour passed. With tears running down her cheeks the loving mother watched her little daughter breathe her last. Jesus had not come! Why?

Something had happened on the way. While Jesus was on His way to Jairus' house, a poor woman who had been very sick for twelve years had pushed her way through the crowd and, stretching her arm between those who were standing close to Jesus, had touched the hem of His garment. Immediately her sickness had been cured, and Jesus had called her to Him to hear her story.

While they were talking together a messenger stepped up to Jairus, who was in the crowd, bringing him the sad news of his daughter's death.

"Thy daughter is dead; trouble not the Master."

Poor Jairus was grief stricken, but Jesus quickly noticed his sorrow. He knew what had happened. Turning to Jairus, He said, "Fear not, believe only, and she shall be made whole."

When Jesus reached Jairus' house He found it full of mourners, who were weeping and wailing and making a terrible noise.

"Why make ye this ado?" He said. "The damsel is not dead, but sleepeth."

At this they all scoffed, because they knew that the girl was dead. Jesus, however, commanded that all except the family should be put outside the door, and this was done.

Then, when all was quiet, He went into the room where the daughter was lying, all white and still. With Him went the sad parents and three of His disciples.

What is He going to do? thought the parents. What *can* He do now? They were very soon to see.

Taking the little girl by the hand, Jesus said to her, "My little daughter, I say unto thee, arise."

The little girl stirred and opened her eyes. Then she got up off the bed just as if she had awakened out of sleep, and looking as well as she had ever been before.

88   As for the parents, they were "astonished with a great astonishment," but I am sure they were wonderfully happy.

And what do you suppose Jesus said then?

"Give her something to eat."

And that just shows that Jesus understands exactly what girls and boys need the most and like the best.

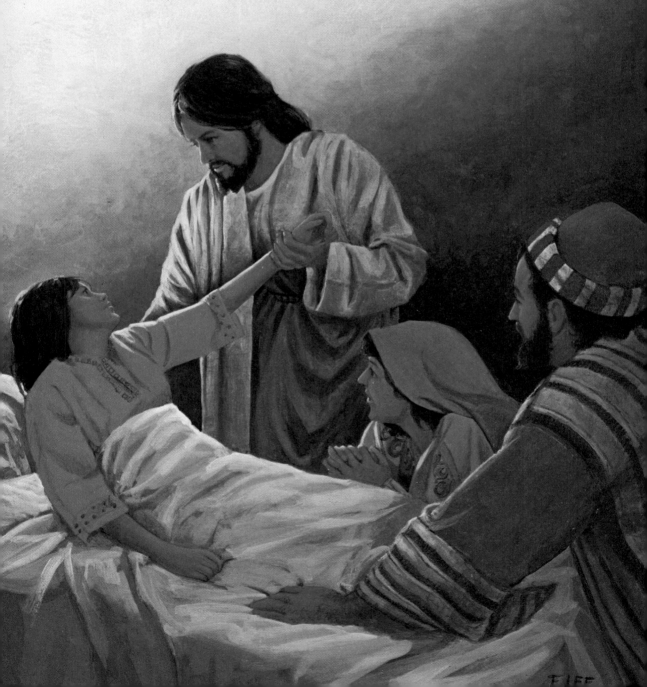

17

The
Wake-up Man

CLAUDE TERRY WORKED in a fine old restaurant in one of the Southern cities of the United States.

The place was open twenty-four hours a day, and Mr. Terry was the night cashier. He began his work between eight and nine o'clock in the evening and went home between six and seven in the morning.

I met him some time ago, and he told me his story.

It all began many years ago. A customer said to him, "Seeing you will be up all night, would you be so kind as to call me in the morning? Here's my telephone number."

"Of course," said Mr. Terry. "I'll be glad to."

The man was so pleased at Mr. Terry's kindness that he told a friend of his who needed to be called early. Mr. Terry said he would be glad to call him, too.

Gradually the idea spread. Pretty soon he was calling ten people every morning. Then fifteen. Then twenty, thirty, forty, fifty! Imagine the time it must have taken him! But Mr. Terry never complained.

Nor did he turn down anybody's request. If a man wanted to be called in the morning, all he had to do was to leave his

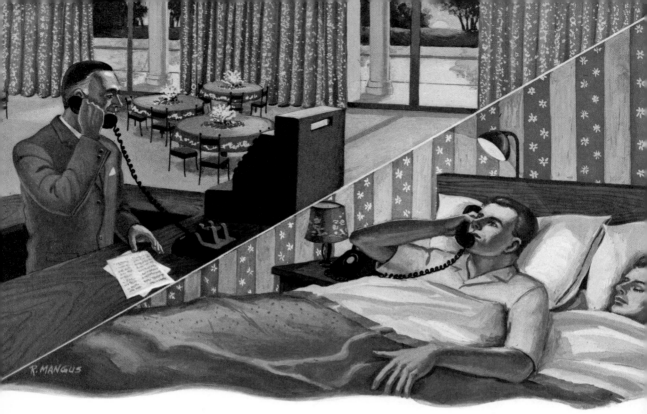

name and telephone number with Mr. Terry, and without fail he would be called on time.

As the years passed, Mr. Terry became known all over town as the "wake-up man."

After I had said good-by to him I couldn't help thinking of Somebody Else who is going to be the "wake-up Man" for people all over the world. You know who I mean.

When Jesus was talking to poor Martha, whose brother Lazarus had just died, He said, "I am the resurrection, and the life: he that believeth in me, though he were dead, yet shall he live." John 11:25. Then He went to the tomb where Lazarus had been buried and called, "Lazarus, come forth!" Lazarus heard His voice, got up, and walked out.

So it was with the widow's son who was being taken to the cemetery in a funeral procession. Jesus told the people who were carrying the body to stop. Then He said, "Young man, get up!" And he did.

It was like that, too, when the little daughter of Jairus

died. Jesus went to see her and found the room full of weeping women. After putting them all outside, He said, "Little girl, get up!" And she did. Mark 5:41.

Someday, the Bible says, *all* who are in their graves shall hear His voice. John 5:28, 29. Isn't that wonderful! It means that Jesus is going to wake up everybody from the sleep of death.

How will this happen? A very famous man has told us. In one of his letters the apostle Paul wrote: "The Lord himself shall descend from heaven with a shout, with the voice of the archangel, and with the trump of God: and the dead in Christ shall rise first: then we which are alive and remain shall be caught up together with them in the clouds, to meet the Lord in the air: and so shall we ever be with the Lord." 1 Thessalonians 4:16, 17.

What a lovely thought! All who have been parted from dear ones by death will be brought together again. Together! Forever!

When will it be? On the "morning" when Jesus comes back again. Then His glorious voice will be heard all around the world, and everybody who went to sleep loving Him will hear it and wake up, never to sleep again.

How comforting it is to think of Jesus as "the wake-up Man"! He won't forget anybody; not grandpas or grandmas or mothers or daddies or brothers or sisters. He will call everybody who has asked Him to, right on time.

Jesus' rising from the tomb gives us the assurance that all who love Him will also come forth from their graves in the resurrection.
Painting by Russell Harlan © by Review and Herald

How Dozy Joe Woke Up

THE TEACHER HAD her eye on Joe. There was something the matter with him, but what it was she could not make out.

There he was again with his eyes shut and his head on his hands, and it was only ten o'clock in the morning!

"Joe, wake up!" she called, and Joe sat up with a start.

"Yes, Miss Lambert," he said, looking at his book again. But it was no use. He couldn't get any meaning out of the words, and his head *would* keep nodding.

Joe was always sleepy; at least, so it seemed to his teacher. And the children in the class thought the same; they called him "Dozy Joe." Sometimes he was too sleepy even to play.

As for his schoolwork, his grades in almost every subject were going from excellent to fair to poor.

Next time Miss Lambert sent a report to Joe's mother she added a few remarks. "Joe is always sleepy," she wrote. "He does not seem able to do good work. I fear there may be something the matter with his health. Perhaps he should see a doctor."

"The idea!" said Joe's mother. "There's nothing the matter with my Joe." All the same, she made up her mind to watch Joe for a while to see whether anything was wrong with him. "Maybe," she said to herself, "I haven't been keeping my eye on him as much as I should."

Mother noticed that when Joe arrived from school he went straight to turn on the TV.

Mother didn't think much of this, for she had often seen Joe watching TV. But an hour later she saw him still there.

"Joe," she said, "haven't you looked at TV long enough?"

"Oh," said Joe, "there's a great show on, about a fight between a plane and a submarine. Can't you hear the guns?"

"Well, Joe, don't stay there too long."

"All right, Mother," said Joe. Another half hour passed.

"Joe!" cried Mother. "Didn't you hear me? Supper's ready."

"I'll be there in a minute," said Joe.

"Come this minute!"

Slowly Joe made his way to the table. As soon as he finished eating he began to slip away to the TV again.

"Where are you going?" asked Mother.

"There's another program coming on in a minute," said Joe. "It's going to be great!"

"But don't you have some homework?"

"I know," said Joe. "I'll do it just as soon as this show is over. It's a series I've been watching every night."

"No," said Mother, "homework first. I want to see it done by the time I get back from Mrs. Jones's."

An hour later, when Mother returned, Joe was still in front of the TV. He jumped up, looking guilty.

"Joe!" cried Mother. "What did I tell you? You've been watching TV the whole time. How can you do your homework now?"

"I'll get it done all right," said Joe with a big yawn.

"You can't," said Mother. "You are too sleepy. You won't learn a thing. You might as well go to bed."

"O.K.," said Joe, yawning again.

But after she went to bed she saw a faint flicker of light under the living room door. She tiptoed to the door and opened it. "Joe! What are you doing here?" she demanded.

"I had to watch this program," said Joe.

"No, you didn't," said Mother. "It wasn't that important. What's more, you have had enough programs to last you for a long time. You can't hope to watch TV at all hours and then do a good job with your schoolwork. You are just making yourself stupid. So that's why you are so sleepy at school."

"I don't think so."

"But I do," Mother said. "We'll keep the TV turned off for a while. Then we can see what happens."

"You mean I can't watch anything anymore?"

"That's exactly what I do mean," said Mother. "You will do no more TV watching until your grades pick up."

"Oh!" groaned Joe.

For a whole month the TV set was kept turned off when Joe was at home. He spent more time on his studies and went to bed early.

Soon a note came from his teacher: "Joe is showing marked improvement and a new interest in his work. He is busy and seems happier." Joe had to admit to himself that it was true. He was happier in school, and somehow he had new energy for his play as well. He was allowed to watch TV again, at reasonable times.

Soon he began to plan to do well in high school and to go on to college someday.

"I want to be somebody when I grow up," he said.

"You're not dozy anymore," said Joe's mother. "When God looks for someone to do something big for Him, He never picks a lazy man. He chooses a busy man."

As Joe began to think of this, the new idea grew slowly but surely in his mind. "I want to be one of God's busy men too."

STORY **19**

Rescue by Airplane

THIS IS A DIFFERENT kind of story from the others in this book, but I want to tell it to you because it is about one of those good-will deeds that make for peace and friendship among the nations of the world.

Some years ago two Spanish airmen set out from Cairo, Egypt, to fly to Baghdad, in Iraq. The journey was dangerous, because the greater part of the flight had to be made across wide deserts where it was impossible to get either food or water in the event of a forced landing.

For some time the two men flew on without trouble, but when crossing the Syrian Desert they lost their way. Finally they ran out of gasoline and had to land on the sand.

They had about three days' supply of food with them, so they waited for some time, hoping that they would be seen by other passing planes. But they were so far off course that there was no possible chance of anyone's coming near them. All day they kept their eyes on the sky, hoping for rescue, but in vain.

It was terribly hot, and they had no shade except what they could get under the wings of their plane. The next day their water began to give out, and they were faced with the terror of slowly dying from thirst. At last they decided to set out on foot in one last effort to find help.

Meanwhile radio messages had been passing between Baghdad and Cairo. Cairo inquired whether the Spanish airmen had arrived safely, and the people at Baghdad replied that they had heard nothing of them. As time passed, everybody began to get anxious.

On the morning of the third day the men in charge of British Royal Air Force units stationed in Egypt decided to send out eight planes in search of the two lost Spaniards. They did not stop to ask from what country they came; they were just brothers in distress.

For four days the eight British planes flew over the length and breadth of the Syrian Desert, the airmen looking down with straining eyes for the lost plane. On the afternoon of the fourth day it was sighted, but to the dismay of the rescuers, the two Spaniards were not there.

Weary and famished, with blistered feet and parched tongue, the Spanish captain trudged on across the sand. It was the sixth day after his forced descent. His water flask had long since been emptied, and he had no more food. He had left his mechanic miles behind, while he looked for help.

The wind had risen, sweeping clouds of sand across the desert, making it hard to see where he was going. He stumbled on like a man in the dark. Would help never come?

100   Listen! What was that? A familiar sound seemed to be coming nearer and nearer. Surely it was the droning of a plane. With new hope he looked up.

He was right. A moment later down from the skies dropped one of the British planes. Just in the nick of time he was rescued.

Then they went back and found the mechanic. They discovered that he had wandered twenty-five miles, and the captain forty-five miles, from their airplane!

Then the news reached Spain, and the story was told in the newspapers how the British airmen had searched for days through blinding sandstorms for the two lost Spaniards. The government expressed its gratitude, and the British embassy at Madrid received thousands of messages, saying how much the people of Spain admired the bravery and chivalry of the British.

So both countries were drawn closer together by this good deed in the desert. And is not this much better than war and fighting and endless faultfinding? Of course it is, and if only men of all nations would always try to be kind and helpful to one another, how much happier a place this world would be!

Painting by Russell Harlan

Russ Harlan

God in the Blueberries

MOTHER WAS OUT of work and greatly in need of money. Suddenly she remembered the blueberries on Farmer Jackson's property, and his need of pickers.

"Would you children like to go with me to pick blueberries?" she asked Ben and Amy. "We could earn a little money that way."

"Of course we'd like to! When can we begin?"

"Tomorrow, maybe," said Mother.

"But tomorrow's Friday," said Amy.

"I know," said Mother, "but we'll begin if we can, even though it is the end of the week."

Early next morning all three were out at the blueberry patch, picking away as hard as they could. Ben and Amy were thrilled to think they could help Mother like this, and they hoped they would have a lot of money to give her at the end of the day. They never grumbled once, no matter how tired they felt as the afternoon wore on.

By and by Farmer Jackson drove up in his truck and loaded on the boxes of blueberries, paying for them on the spot.

Amy received about $1.50, Ben about $2.00, and Mother a little bit more. All were grateful and happy. It had been a good day, and now they had money enough to buy groceries for the weekend.

"It will be lovely to get home again and clean up," said Mother.

"Could we go by the creek?" asked Ben.

"Surely," said Mother, "if you don't mind the extra walk."

The children said they didn't mind, so off they all went through the blueberry patch to the creek. They had almost reached the bank when Amy gave a cry of alarm.

"My purse!" she cried. "Where is it?"

"Oh! You haven't lost it, have you?" asked Mother anxiously.

"I don't know," said Amy. "I had it only a few minutes ago, but it's gone. I must have dropped it somewhere."

"And it had all your money in it." Mother looked sad.

"Yes," said Amy. "A dollar and fifty cents. I never had so much money before."

"And we need it so badly," said Mother. "Come, let's look for it."

But the grass was long and the berry patch thick, and it was like looking for a needle in a haystack.

They searched for an hour without success. They looked everywhere, even in the creek, but found no trace of the purse.

Now the sun was getting low in the sky and they knew it would soon be dark. Hungry, weary, and discouraged, they stood for a moment wondering what to do next. Mother and Ben said they should go home and leave the purse, but Amy thought they should stay and take one more look.

"Don't you think we should kneel down and ask God to help us?" she asked.

"Maybe we should," said Mother. "Let's do it."

So they knelt there in the blueberry patch and told God all about their trouble, and how they needed His help right then and there, before darkness should fall.

"Please, dear God," said Amy, "help me to find my purse. You know where it is. Do tell us. Then we can go home happy."

Mother said Amen. So did Ben. And both hoped with all their hearts that God would answer Amy's prayer.

Then they all stood up and searched some more. But all in vain.

"I'm afraid we'll have to go, dear," said Mother. "It's getting so late. It's too bad, I know, and I'm so sorry——"

But she never finished the sentence, for all of a sudden she shouted, "There it is!"

Amy's purse was right at her feet, a yard or so from the creek. She had nearly stepped on it.

"Now we must have another prayer meeting," said Amy, "and thank God for being so good to us."

They did. Right there in the blueberry patch.

21

How Polly
Came to Stay

SOME YEARS AGO Farmer Norman was driving the milk truck into town one cold winter morning when he heard a strange squealing sound coming from the gutter beside the road. Stopping his truck, he went over to investigate, and what do you suppose he found? You would never guess. Two little puppies, so small they looked as though they were only just born!

As he was wondering how they came to be there and what he should do with them, a woman came up. She had heard the squealing, too, and wondered what it was all about.

"Too bad to treat little pups like that!" she said. "Poor little things!"

"Looks as though someone has thrown them out to die," said Mr. Norman. "What shall we do with them?"

"I don't know," said the woman, "but if you'll look after one, I'll take the other."

"All right," said Mr. Norman, picking up the smaller puppy. "Guess I had better wrap it up, or it might die of cold."

Finding he had nothing in his truck to use as a covering, he took off his coat, put it carefully around the puppy, and set

106

out for home.

"What in the world have you got there?" asked Mrs. Norman, looking at the strange bundle he was bringing into the house.

Mr. Norman unwrapped his coat, revealing the tiny puppy. Mother exploded.

"What are you up to now, Ralph?" she said. "What do you mean by bringing that thing home? It's too small. It will be too much trouble to feed."

"But I couldn't leave it out on the road to die," said Mr. Norman. "At least, we can feed it once."

Just then little Clare ran up. "Oh, what a dear, sweet little puppy!" she cried. "Is it ours? Oh, do let us keep it, Mother."

They kept it. After Mother had fed it a few times, she began to like the little thing.

At first nobody could tell just what kind of dog it was. Of course, they knew it wasn't a cocker spaniel, because it

didn't have the right kind of ears. And
it didn't look as though it could ever
grow up to be a collie or a greyhound
or a Saint Bernard. What was it?
Maybe just a mongrel of no particular
kind at all.

They called the pup Polly, and before long she was the pet of the whole
family.

One day as Mother looked out the
window, she saw Polly playing with a
gopher, a sort of distant cousin to a rat,
which does all kinds of damage in a
garden. "Catch it!" she said, and Polly
did.

Nearly every morning after that
Polly would catch another gopher. She
came to be the best gopher catcher anyone could wish to have. Whenever she
caught one she would lay it on the
porch until Mother would come and see

it. Then she would wag her tail as though saying, "There you are! See! I've caught another for you." And by the way she wiggled her whole body it was plain she was mighty pleased with her little self.

One day the cows broke out of the pasture. The men were away, and Mother didn't know what to do. Could Polly help to bring them back? She had never done it before. Mother decided to try. Polly, though still only a puppy, caught on at once. She kept the cows from straying till help arrived. Every day after that she rounded up the cows and brought them in for milking, just as though she had done it for years. Sometimes in very rainy weather she had to swim a stream to get to the cows, then drive them back through the stream to the barn. But she never hesitated. All Mother had to say was, "Fetch the cows, Polly!" and off Polly went and fetched them. She never failed.

There never was such an intelligent dog. She knew just what to do when tramps came near the house. She had her own way of showing them to the gate and suggesting that they should

not come back. Maybe it was the way her hair stood up, or the way she bared her teeth. Anyway, they seemed to understand perfectly.

On school days Polly would go with Clare as far as the school bus. If the bus was late, she would sit on top of a tree stump looking for it, while Clare read a book at her side. In the afternoon she met the bus when Clare came home. She never missed.

Then one day poor Polly got a foxtail spine in her ear. No one thought much of it at first, but by and by the ear began to fester. She was taken to a veterinarian, who did all he could to make her better, but it was no use. Polly grew worse, and her pain became so great that the doctor at last decided that the kindest thing to do was to put her to sleep.

What a sad day that was for everybody! Mother cried, Clare cried, even Father shed a tear or two. It was hard to believe that they had all come to care so much for the little stray pup that Father had found in the gutter. How much happiness that one kindly deed had brought to them all!

22

A Bit Too Fast

NIGEL WAS SHOUTING for joy all over the house. Everything else had to come to a standstill till the good news had been told.

"Mother! Father! Nellie! I've got a fire truck. I've got a fire truck!"

"What's this? What's this?" called Mother, somewhat confused by the noise.

"I've got a fire truck, Mother. Come and see it."

So the family walked outside to see the great sight. And there it was—at the bottom of the kitchen steps—a pedal fire truck, with a bell and a ladder and bright-red paint. No wonder Nigel was happy. True, the paint was scratched here and there, but what did Nigel care about that? He had his fire truck, and what else mattered?

"Where did you get it?" asked Father sternly.

"Oh, Billy, the boy next door, sold it to me. Cost only five dollars. Paid for it myself—you said I could spend my own savings." He stopped at the look on his father's face, then went on, "Boy, oh boy, she's a beauty, don't you think, Father?"

111

"Pretty nice," said Father, "but where are you going to play with it?"

"Oh, around the house and on the sidewalk," said Nigel. "And if Nellie promises to be good, I'll take her with me sometimes."

"I'll be good," cried Nellie. "Let's go now."

"Come on, then," said Nigel, and they both climbed in.

"Just a minute," said Father. "Be careful. Keep on the sidewalk in front of the house and around the block. Don't go on the hill, and don't go too fast."

"Oh, we'll be all right," said Nigel, and off they went. They had a grand time and came back in an hour, tired out but happy. Nigel thought that pushing the pedals down was a bit hard on his legs, but he loved it anyway.

Again and again the two went out together, driving the truck all around the block. Nigel began to get more and more sure of himself. He pushed the truck across the street and rode on the opposite sidewalk.

"We're still in front of the house," he said, "only on the other side of the street." Then he became less and less satisfied at going so slowly.

"Let's ride around this block too," he said as he turned the corner. "I believe we could start going downhill now."

"Remember what Father said," Nellie reminded him.

"I know," he said, "but that was when we were just starting. He wouldn't mind now. And it's only a little hill here."

"If it's only a little hill," said Nellie, "I don't suppose it will matter."

Then he turned the second corner, because the sidewalk still had only a gentle slope on River Drive. What fun it was to glide down it! This is grand! thought Nigel.

But when he turned the third corner, they both had to get out and push the truck up the long, winding, steep slope to get back.

Now they wanted still more excitement.

"Let's go around the block the other way," said Nigel, "so we can ride down the steep part instead of pushing the truck up it."

"You mean that way?" Nellie pointed to the steep slope they had just walked up, with the river at the bottom.

"Sure, that one," said Nigel, laughing at her fear.

"Could we manage that?" asked Nellie, a little scared. "Would we stop in time?"

"Of course we would. This truck of mine does just what I want it to do. It couldn't run away from *me*."

"What will Father say when he finds out we've been down that hill?"

"Oh, he wouldn't care," said Nigel. "Anyway, he won't know."

So off they went, down the forbidden hill. At first the road was flat, or gently sloping; then it turned down more steeply, winding this way and that until it reached River Drive at the bottom. Nigel was sure it would be lots of fun to guide his truck around those curves. It would be easier if he drove in the road, since the sidewalk was so narrow.

As they drove down the first long, gentle slope, everything went fine. Nigel and Nellie laughed and yelled for
joy. Then as the road got steeper and began to curve, Nellie
became anxious, and the smile left her face.

"Oh, do be careful!" she cried as they rounded a curve
on two wheels. "You nearly threw me out."

"Don't worry," cried Nigel. "This is fun. Don't you like
it, Nellie?"

"N-n-n-n-n-no!" cried Nellie, gripping Nigel around the
neck and holding on for dear life. "Stop it, stop it!"

"Can't stop yet," called Nigel, just managing to get
around the next bend without turning over. "Got to keep
going now till we get to the bottom."

Whoosh! they rounded another curve.

"Ooh!" cried Nellie. "Stop it! Stop it! Please stop it,
Nigel!"

"Wish I could," cried Nigel, who was beginning to get anxious himself now. "My feet slipped off the pedals—can't get them on again—moving too fast."

Whoosh! Another curve, but still they were on the road and right side up. Nigel was at least doing a good job of steering.

Then they rounded another curve, and right in front of them was River Drive and the dirt road beyond.

"Ooh!" cried Nellie. "The river! Watch out!"

Just as if he could stop!

Nigel had no choice.

The truck rolled across River Drive, onto the dirt road, and down the bank. It hit the water and overturned, throwing both of them into the river. Fortunately the water was not deep, and they were able to crawl out again without serious harm. But what a sight they were!

Just then a car came down the hill, and a horn blew loudly. Then a voice, loud and stern and strangely familiar, burst on their ears. They were frozen with surprise.

"Nigel! Nellie! What in the world are you doing here?"

It was Father!

He jumped out and pushed them both into the car, throwing the fire truck into the trunk. Then he sped home as fast as he could, lest they should catch cold.

"Nigel," he said, as they drew near the house, "when will you learn to take advice? I told you to keep on the sidewalk and to avoid hills, and I knew what I was talking about. And yet you took this truck down the worst hill in the district, with Nellie on it, too! I never heard of such foolishness. You might both have been drowned or run into by a car on those curves."

"I'm sorry," said Nigel. "I won't go on the hill again."

"You certainly won't!" said Father. "That fire truck is going in the garage *now,* and it is going to stay there until you are old enough and sensible enough to do what you are told."

"Oh, no!" cried Nigel.

"Oh, yes!" said Father.

And into the garage the little fire truck went—until Nigel was a wiser and a better boy.

23

The Treasure Hunt

IT HAD BEEN a dreary, wet afternoon, with the rain coming down in bucketfuls. And from the way it was still coming down, the children thought it would go on raining forever and ever.

Everybody was about as miserable as he could be, and a bit short-tempered too, if the truth must be told.

The children had played every game they could think of, and now there just didn't seem to be anything else to do.

It was when things were getting as gloomy inside as they were outside that Mother came along with one of her bright ideas.

"I'll tell you what," she said cheerfully. "Let's have a treasure hunt."

There was a chorus of approval.

"Good idea!" shouted Wilfred. "What shall we hunt?"

"Will there be a prize?" cried Sylvia.

"Anything for a change," gasped Gilbert from his seat on the sofa. "Let's begin."

"I want to hunt too," cried Baby. "Let me hunt, Mommy."

118   "All in good time," said Mother. "Now listen. I have hid-

den a treasure somewhere in this house, and I'm going to give you fifteen minutes to find it. The one who finds it will win the cake I've bought for supper."

"Good!" said Wilfred. "I'm going to find it then."

"But what is it like?" asked Sylvia. "We don't know anything about it yet."

"Well," said Mother mysteriously, "it's not very small and it's not very big."

"But that's not telling us enough. We might bring anything," said Gilbert.

"I know," Mother went on. "But this particular object is the most valuable thing in the house, and you have to think what this is before you begin to look."

"Um," said Wilfred, frowning. "What can it be? I didn't think there was anything very valuable in this house. Is it the old grandfather clock?"

"No," said Mother, "of course not, and please don't try to bring that in here. And I'll tell you this: It's squarish but not square, and it's more than an inch wide and less than a foot long. It's not locked, but when you open it you will find lots of valuable things inside."

"Oh, I can't imagine what it is!" exclaimed Gilbert lazily.

"Think, then," said Mother. "I'm going to begin counting in just a minute from now. And mind, if you look in any cupboards or drawers, you must leave everything exactly as you find it. If you don't, you'll lose the prize anyway. Now away you all go. One, two, thrrreeeee!"

Away they went.

Gilbert hurried to the cupboard where he remembered Father kept the little black box with some precious papers inside. But it was locked, so he went off on another scent.

Wilfred hunted upstairs, crawling under all the beds, with Baby at his heels, enjoying the fun immensely.

Bang! bang! bang! went the cupboard doors as one by one they were opened and closed.

Sylvia wandered about quietly with a thoughtful look on her face.

"Now, what can it be?" she said to herself. "The most valuable thing in the house? Um. It can't be money, for there isn't much of that. And it can't be jewelry, for Mother hasn't any. Um. It might be a picture, but it isn't more than a foot long, and we haven't any pictures that size. Um. It might be one of those queer curios on the mantelpiece in the parlor, but hardly so, for it's something that can be opened. Yes, opened. What things can be opened? Boxes and bags and brief cases and, um, yes, books!"

Why, there was an idea. Why hadn't she thought of that before?

It might be one of the old books in the bookcase. She hurried over to it.

"Three more minutes!" called Mother from the kitchen.

"I've got something," cried Gilbert.

"So have I," shouted Wilfred, his voice seeming to come from the attic.

"And so have I," echoed Baby from the same quarter.

Feverishly Sylvia looked along the rows of books, but which one to choose she could not tell. Many of the titles she did not even recognize. There were books on history, astronomy, literature, and all sorts of things, with here and there a big fat dictionary. Suddenly, just between two of these large volumes she spied a smaller one, and a happy smile spread across her face.

"Got it!" she said to herself, as she picked it out and hurried with it to the dining room.

"Time!" called Mother.

Down came the others helter-skelter.

"Well, what have you found for me?" asked Mother.

"Your purse," said Gilbert.

Mother laughed. "So you think that's the most valuable thing in this house! Well, it isn't, by a long, long way, especially at the end of the week."

"I think I've got it," said Wilfred, bringing out a dusty, old-fashioned mother-of-pearl box he had found in the attic.

"Well, I never!" exclaimed Mother. "How did you find that? I haven't seen it for years and years. It belonged to my grandmother, and it is very precious to me; yet it isn't the most valuable thing that I hid specially and wanted you to find."

Wilfred looked rather disappointed.

"And what did you bring, Baby dear?" asked Mother.

"Just me," said Baby, at which, of course, Mother had to pick him up and hug him for a full minute.

"You surely are the sweetest thing," she said, kissing him. "But has nobody found what I hid?"

Sylvia felt sure she had discovered the treasure, and at this moment produced her find.

"Well done!" cried Mother. "Sylvia has won! What made you think of it?"

"I don't know," said Sylvia. "I just saw it and guessed."

"Who'd have thought of that!" exclaimed Gilbert. "A Bible!"

"Yes," said Mother. "And I wonder why you didn't all think of it together. Of course it's the most valuable thing in this house. When you open it, you find it is full of the richest treasure. It is a gold mine of truth, full of beautiful stories of Jesus and His love. There is wonderful counsel

here to keep us from making mistakes, from doing things
we might be sorry for, and to tell us how to share at last in
all the riches and glory of God's eternal kingdom. Why,
there's nothing more precious."

"But you can buy it for a dollar," said Gilbert.

"I know," said Mother. "But remember, when one of the
early copies of this Book was sold some years ago, it took
five hundred thousand dollars to buy it. Only the Bible
could have brought such a price. Printing has made it cheap
for us to buy, but it is just as precious inside as it ever
was."

"Wish I'd thought of that," said Wilfred, looking woe-
fully at the supper table.

"Never mind," said Sylvia gracefully. "I'll cut that cake
into five pieces and share it with everybody."

"Mother," said Wilfred, "will you read us a Bible story
after supper?"

"I certainly will," said Mother. "We'll open the treasure
chest and enjoy some of the treasures that have been put in
it for us."

24

Myrtle's
Sad Mistake

THERE WAS ONE THING that Myrtle could never bring herself to do, and that was to own up when she had done something wrong. From the time she was a very little girl till now, when she was almost ten years old, she just *couldn't* do it. Whenever she did something that she knew she shouldn't have done, instead of owning up to it right away, she would make up some story that she thought would excuse herself and cover up her mistake.

Of course, it wasn't any good. Mother always found out. However much she lied, Mother always got the truth out of her at last, and then there was always the penalty to pay, which wasn't very pleasant.

But though Myrtle had told dozens of stories like this, and had been found out just as many dozens of times, she still kept on telling them with the same sad results. Then one day something happened that changed everything.

It was Christmas, and when Myrtle opened her presents, what should she find but the dearest, prettiest little watch she had ever seen! She was too happy for words. Never had she dared to hope that Mother and Dad would give her any-

thing so beautiful, and this in addition to all her other presents too.

Myrtle put the watch on her wrist and gazed at it by the hour. To think that it was a real one that kept proper time, and not just a dime-store toy, such as she had had before! How the girls at school would envy her!

Of course, Mother and Dad told her to be very careful with such an expensive gift. She was to wind it slowly, and never overwind it. She was to take it off her wrist before she washed her hands or the dishes. And, of course, she must take it off before she had a shower or a bath.

"If you take good care of that little watch," Dad said, "it may serve you until you go through college."

"Oh, I'll take care of it," said Myrtle. "Trust me to do that. I wouldn't let any harm come to it for worlds! It is the most beautiful thing I ever owned."

Then one evening, about a month later, Myrtle was having her bath. She had done her hair and washed herself all over when she suddenly noticed that her precious watch was still on her wrist. Sick with fright, she leaped out of the tub,

removed the watch, and held it to her ear. It had stopped!

"Oh!" she cried. "My lovely little watch! I've ruined it. I've ruined it!"

Then came the dreadful thought, What will Mother say? What will Dad say? She felt she could not face them. Kind and loving though they were, she thought she simply could not tell them the terrible truth about what she had done.

But what to do? If she did not wear the watch, they would wonder why. And if she did wear it and they noticed it had stopped, they would be bound to question her. She decided to make up a story about it and hope that they would not ask about the watch till she had thought it all out so carefully they would never suspect what had really happened.

A number of days passed, during which Myrtle kept her secret to herself. Then at breakfast one morning Dad asked her the time.

"I'm not quite sure," she said, blushing just a little. "I'm afraid my watch has stopped."

"Stopped?" said Dad. "Surely not. Did you forget to wind it last night?"

"Oh, no, no," said Myrtle. "I wound it all right, but—well —it just stopped."

"Let me see it," said Dad.

Myrtle took it off her wrist and handed it to him.

"Strange," said Dad. "It looks a little misty under the glass. I wonder what could have caused that?"

"I was wondering too," said Myrtle. "Perhaps I got it wet when I was out in the rain last night. But I didn't think the rain could get through the glass."

"I should not think so," said Dad. "I'll have another look at this when I get home this evening."

When Dad had gone, Mother asked to see the watch. She too noticed the mistiness under the glass.

"Very strange," she said. "I can see little drops of water in there, too. Myrtle, are you sure you had this watch out in the rain?"

"Oh, yes, Mother, yes. It was raining quite hard."

"No. Not last night," said Mother, getting a little suspicious. "It didn't rain last night at all."

"Then it must have been the night before," said Myrtle, blushing deeper still.

"Are you quite sure that the water in this watch is rain water?"

"Oh, yes—er—yes—I think it must be," said Myrtle.

"Are you sure it is not bath water?" asked Mother very sternly.

"No—er—yes—er—no; I'm not quite sure," said Myrtle, now very upset.

"Tell me the truth, Myrtle! Did you get into the tub with this watch on your wrist?"

Myrtle saw that there was no use trying to deceive Mother any longer. She gave in.

"Yes," she said, "I did."

"Then why did you tell me all this story about going out in the rain with it on?"

"Because I was afraid of what you and Dad would say to me."

"When did you do this?"

"Last week—Monday night, I think."

"Why, that's too long ago! Oh, if only you had told me right away, instead of lying about it all this time!"

"Why?"

"Because if you had told me at once, I would have rushed the watch to the jeweler's, and he would have dried it immediately, and no harm would have come to it. Now it must be all rusty inside and probably will never go again."

"Never go again!" sobbed poor Myrtle. "Oh, if only I had told you at once! Why did I ever lie about it? Now I have lost my beautiful watch forever."

It was a hard, hard lesson that Myrtle learned that day. But I am glad to tell you that she did learn it. In the future, whenever she was tempted to cover up a mistake with a false story, she remembered what had happened to her precious watch and decided to own up and tell the truth right away.

25

Alan's "Sandwich"

CHRISTMAS WAS SEVERAL months away on that beautiful summer morning when six-year-old Alan walked into one of the lovely parks in the city where he lived. As a matter of fact, he wasn't thinking about Christmas at all. Nor did it enter his head that what he would do that day would bring so much happiness to many people on the next December 25.

All he could think about at the moment was the fact that he was hungry. So hungry, indeed, that he began to wonder whether he had forgotten to eat his breakfast. He wished he had brought some lunch with him, at least an apple or a few cookies. He searched his pockets, but couldn't find a crumb.

Since the friends he usually played with hadn't turned up, he wandered about looking at the flowers and peering hopefully among the bushes for a bird's nest.

Then it was that he saw the package. It was small, about the size of a sandwich, and wrapped in cellophane. Feeling sure it must be a sandwich, he picked it up eagerly, hoping ants hadn't gotten inside and spoiled it.

129

Through the cellophane it surely looked like a sandwich.
It was green inside, and you couldn't blame a hungry boy
for thinking it was something to eat. But it wasn't a sandwich. No indeed. It was money. Lots of money! Alan had
never seen so much before. Not in all his life.

In his excitement he forgot all about being hungry. But
he was puzzled as to what to do next.

His first thought was to run home and show his mother
what he had found. Then he remembered something she
had told him some time before.

"If you ever find anything that does not belong to you,"
she had said, "take it to a police station at once. The owner
will probably be looking for it and will be very glad to get
it back again. This will be doing to others as you would like
them to do to you."

Alan thought about that a moment. Then he made up
his mind.

Putting the package in his pocket, he ran to the nearest
police station, which was not very far from the park gates.
He pushed open the big glass door, then hesitated.

"What can I do for you, sonny?" asked the big policeman
at the desk.

"Please, sir, I found something," said Alan. "It looks like
money."

The policeman took the package.

"Whew!" he whistled as he counted out two hundred and
ten dollars. "It surely is money. Where did you find this?"

Alan told his story.

"Thank you," said the policeman. "Thank you very
much. We like honest boys such as you. We will keep the
package here a few weeks and see if anybody claims it. If
nobody does, it will be given back to you."

"To me?" cried Alan excitedly.

"That's the law," said the policeman. "But don't get your
hopes up too high. Usually people who lose a large amount

◀ Painting by Russell Harlan © by Review and Herald

**"Please, sir," said Alan to the big policeman at
the desk, "I found something. It looks like
money."**

of money soon begin asking for it. Give me your name and address."

Alan ran home to tell his mother what had happened.

"I'm proud of you," she said. "You did exactly the right thing. Probably you won't get the money. You may not even get a reward for finding it. But never mind. You did what was honest and good, and that's what matters most."

At this Alan went back to the park, eating the biggest apple Mother could find.

Days, weeks, and months slipped by. Alan's "sandwich" was forgotten. So too was the hope that there might be a reward for finding the money.

October passed. So did November. And most of December.

Only three days remained before Christmas. Mother

should have been feeling very happy. But she wasn't. She had hoped so much that this year she might make this the best Christmas ever for her family. But now she knew she couldn't. There had been just too many bills to pay.

Then came a knock at the front door.

Mother wiped her hands on her apron, brushed back her hair, and hurried to open it. Alan was not far behind her.

They were startled to see a big policeman outside.

"Whatever is the matter?" Mother asked anxiously.

"Nothing really, ma'am," he said kindly. "I believe you have a very honest little boy here."

"I hope so," she said. "You mean my Alan?"

"Yes," he said, producing a package from his pocket. "Some months ago he found this in the park and brought it to the police station."

"It's my 'sandwich'!" Alan yelled with delight.

"Well," said the policeman, "since nobody has claimed it, we will give it to the finder. Please sign this receipt."

Mother signed, and the policeman went on his way. Then what shrieks of joy filled the house!

Part of the money was used to open a savings account for Alan, part went to buy him and his brothers and sisters some much-needed clothes, and part was spent to get everybody some extra-special gifts for Christmas. Alan's "sandwich" proved to be filled with Christmas cheer.

What a Christmas that was! The most wonderful they had ever enjoyed. And all because a little boy had learned to be honest.

STORY **26**

The Shipwrecked Printer

HIRAM BINGHAM had always wanted to be a missionary. Now his dream had come true. He was on his way to the South Sea Islands.

At last, after a long, rough voyage in a sailing ship—for it was the year 1857—he arrived at a lonely spot in the Gilbert Islands.

There he preached and worked for many years, doing his best to win the people to Jesus. But it was a difficult task, for in those days there was no Bible in the language of the people. Every text, every sermon, had to be translated by an interpreter.

Gradually Hiram became more and more familiar with the language. Then he decided that he would translate at least a portion of the Bible, so that the island people could learn to read the Word of God in their own tongue. For a long time he worked on the book of Matthew, trying to make its beautiful message as simple and clear as he could.

At last it was finished. Then came the question, How could he get it printed? There was nobody in all the Gilbert Islands who could do it. Certainly there was no printing press there, not in those days.

The nearest place that the book could be printed was in the Hawaiian Islands, more than two thousand miles away. But Hiram decided that it must be done. So he sent his precious manuscript on the mission ship to a printer in Honolulu. Then he waited and waited for thirteen months before he heard anything more about it. All that time he looked forward eagerly to getting his precious books.

At last the mission ship returned. There were many boxes on board for him, but not a single copy of the Gospel of Matthew! Not one. The manuscript had not been printed! What a disappointment! After all that long, long waiting, too.

Only one thing happened to cheer him at that time. Opening the boxes addressed to him, he found, of all things, a printing press! The people in Hawaii who couldn't print the book had sent him an old hand press with the suggestion that he print it himself.

But Hiram was not a printer. Although he studied the

book of instructions as best he could, he couldn't make head or tail of it. Soon he came to the conclusion that his Gospel of Matthew would never be printed if he had to print it on that press himself. Then how was it to be done? There wasn't anybody in all the Gilbert Islands who knew how a press worked. So there it lay.

Shortly after the mission ship had sailed again, leaving Hiram Bingham with the old press but no Bibles, a strange and wonderful thing happened.

Hiram had prayed much that God would send someone to him who would be able to use the press and to print his precious manuscript of the Gospel of Matthew. Yet it seemed that his prayer could never be answered. Seldom did anyone visit the islands in those days. And why should a printer want to go where people could not read and where no printing press had ever been heard of before? Yet Hiram was sure that someday, in some wonderful way, God would answer.

One morning, looking seaward, he spied a small boat trying to reach the shore. He guessed that it must be a lifeboat from some ship that had been wrecked, and he was right. Then he wondered how many sailors were aboard, and how long they had been at sea in that frail little craft.

Then his heart leaped. Yes! There were signs of life in the boat. Three figures were waving.

Calling some islanders to his aid, he succeeded in bringing the boat to land. The three men aboard were indeed survivors of a shipwreck. Their ship had gone down in a storm six hundred miles away, and they had been sailing ten days in search of an island. The rest of the crew had been drowned.

When the three men had eaten and rested, Mr. Bingham began to talk with them about themselves and their plans for the future. To his amazement one of them said, "I am a printer."

A printer! Only three men saved, and one a printer!

You can imagine how happy and thankful Hiram was when he made this discovery. At once he and his new-found friend began to plan about the printing of the precious manuscript. Mr. Hotchkiss—for that was the printer's name—was sure he could set up the press and, in fact, within a few weeks he had it in working order.

Some time later the first edition of the full Gospel of Matthew in the language of the people of the Gilbert Islands came from that press. One copy of it may still be seen at the head office of the American Bible Society in New York City.

As a result of the printing and preaching of the gospel in those far-off islands, almost the entire population accepted Christ. Today there are many thousands of Christians there. And God saved a printer from a shipwreck to make it possible.

27

The Mark
on Her Foot

PEGGY HAS A MARK on her foot. If you were to go wading with her, or swimming, you would see it. It looks like an old scar. It is. But I doubt that she would tell you how it got there.

It happened when Peggy was a little girl of 5. That was when she became so interested in gardening.

All of a sudden she decided she wanted to have a part of the back garden where she could grow things all on her own.

"If you will let me have a little piece," she said to Mother, "I will dig it and rake it and water it and weed it and everything."

"Aren't you a little young for that?" asked Mother, who didn't want part of her garden to become a wilderness after a while.

"Oh, no," said Peggy. "I'm old enough. And my piece will be the best of all. You'll see."

At last Mother decided to let Peggy have a piece of ground all her own. "But you must look after it properly," she said, "or I'll have to take it back again."

139

Peggy was delighted and dragged Mother out into the garden to mark out her plot.

This done, she took the smallest fork from the tool shed and began to dig. Since there had been a good deal of rain lately, the ground was soft and it turned easily. Peggy thought it was great fun.

Next day she went out and dug some more.

The day after that was Sabbath, and when Peggy got home from church she changed her clothes, took her little fork, and went out to dig some more.

Mother found her there.

"Surely you are not digging today," said Mother.

"Why not?" said Peggy.

"Because it's the Sabbath. You know that. You've just come back from church."

"I know, but why can't I dig my garden today?"

"Because that's working, and we shouldn't do our own work on the Sabbath."

"Why shouldn't we?"

"You know why," said Mother. "God has told us not to."

Then she quoted the fourth commandment: " 'Remember the sabbath day, to keep it holy. Six days shalt thou labour, and do all thy work: but the seventh day is the sabbath of the Lord thy God: in it thou shalt not do any work, thou, nor thy son, nor thy daughter' (Exodus 20:8-10).

"And because you are my daughter," said Mother, "you had better come indoors right now."

Sadly Peggy left her fork sticking in the ground and went back to the house with Mother. On the way she muttered, "I don't see why I can't dig my garden today if I want to."

Mother tried to explain that it isn't good to do *our* work on God's day, but all she said didn't seem to do much good.

Peggy sulked and grumbled and even refused to listen when Mother began to read a Bible story.

By and by, when Mother wasn't looking, she slipped out into the garden and began digging again. That was when it happened.

Being in a bad mood, she couldn't see straight, and so, instead of putting the fork in the ground, she stuck it in her foot. One prong went right through her sneaker into her foot.

What a yell she let out then!

Her frightful screams brought Mother rushing into the garden. She pulled the prong out and carried her indoors. Her mother did not scold as she bound up the wound, but with tender, loving care impressed on her the importance of obedience. Then she took her to the doctor.

Peggy still likes working in her garden, but she does it only six days a week. On the seventh day as she sees the lovely flowers growing from the tiny seeds she has planted, her little heart overflows with happiness and love and she says within herself, "Thank You, dear God, for making such beautiful flowers to grow in my garden. I'll always remember the Sabbath day to keep it holy."

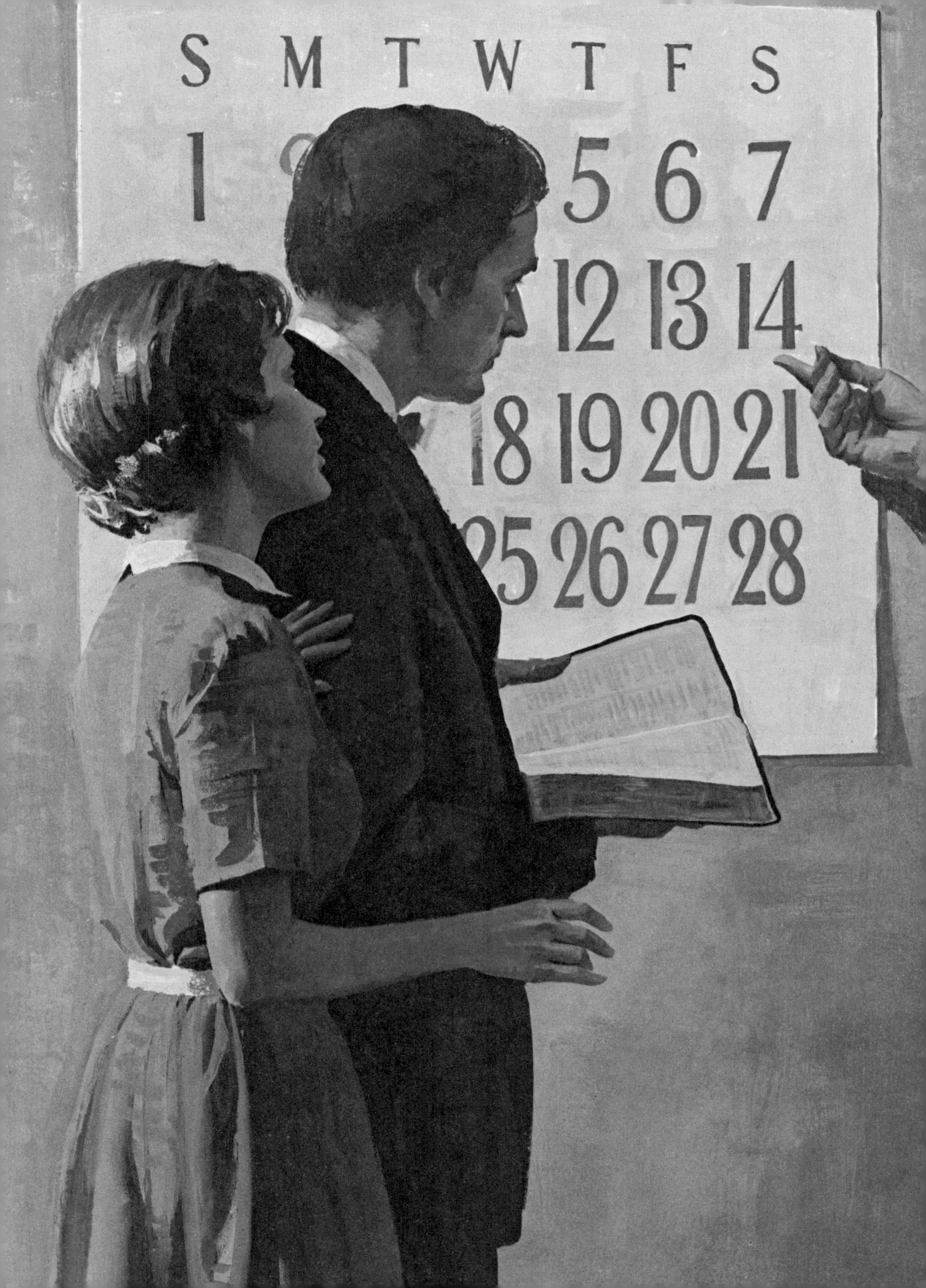
S M T W T F S
1 5 6 7
12 13 14
18 19 20 21
25 26 27 28

28

Boy in a Well

THE WELL WAS 525 feet deep, with the water level about 250 feet from the bottom.

That is a deep well, but it wasn't deep enough for the farmer, who needed great quantities of water for his crops. So he decided to drill the well still deeper.

One day the driller arrived, bringing with him his little boy, Harry, aged 7, who loved to watch while his daddy was at work.

The first job was to remove all the machinery from the top of the well. Then, section by section, the steel rod that held the pumping "bowls" far down in the water was withdrawn. This done, the driller placed a piece of three-ply over the sixteen-inch hole to keep dirt, stones, and small animals from falling in while he was getting the drill ready.

For some reason known only to small boys, Harry thought it would be smart to jump on the piece of three-ply while Daddy was looking the other way.

Suddenly there was a sharp crack followed by a wild scream.

144   Daddy looked around just in time to see Harry disap-

◄ Painting by Harry Anderson © by Review and Herald

The seventh day of the week is very special. God calls it "My holy day." Jesus invites us all to keep the Sabbath as He did.

pear down the well. Rushing to the rim he yelled in anguish, "Harry!"

He was too late to help.

With awful speed poor Harry dropped like a stone, feet first, down that pipe.

Down, down, down he went, two hundred and seventy-five feet!

Daddy rushed to the hole and yelled, "Harry!" never expecting an answer.

Faintly, from far below, an answer came.

"I'm all right, Daddy," called Harry. "Get me out of here."

Evidently the piece of plywood, as it went down beneath him, had compressed the air in the pipe and so had broken his fall. Now he was floating in the dark water with only a pinpoint of light far above him.

Daddy was beside himself with worry and grief.

"I'm going down after him," he cried to the other drillers. "Tie a rope on me and let me down."

"You can't go down there," they said. "Your feet would push him under."

"Then I'll go head first," said Daddy.

"You'd get stuck and both of you would die."

"I suppose so," agreed Daddy. "We'll have to lower a rope."

But there was no rope, only a steel cable.

Frantically Daddy pushed the cable down the well, cutting his hands badly. But the cable merely coiled up in the pipe and had to be pulled out again.

"Can't somebody get a rope!" yelled Daddy desperately, for time was running out.

A man remembered that there was rope and a block and tackle on a ranch seven miles away. He set off at top speed to fetch it.

"How are you, Harry?" Daddy called.

"I'm still all right, but hurry, Daddy, hurry!"

"We're hurrying the best we can, son," cried Daddy. "Hold on! Keep pushing against the sides of the pipe so you won't sink. Don't get scared. We're going to get you out!"

Now the man returned with the rope. He had grabbed every lariat he could find and, tying them together, had made a rope 300 feet long, with a big loop at one end.

Daddy shouted down the well again.

"Harry! There's a rope coming down. Grab the loop and put it under both arms."

"Can't I just hold it?" asked Harry.

"No!" said Daddy. "You couldn't. Do exactly as I say. Put the loop under your arms."

"All right, Daddy."

"Have you got it?"

"Yes."

"Is it under your arms?"

"Yes."

"Then keep it there and hold on!"

Several men began to pull, scared to death lest Harry should fall out of the loop.

Had the boy done exactly as his daddy had told him? Was the rope under both arms, or only under one?

Little by little the rope came up out of the well. Fifty feet, a hundred feet, two hundred feet. All the time Harry's voice became louder and louder. He was coming up too!

As his head appeared at the top, Daddy reached in and grabbed him.

His boy was safe! He was back from almost certain death!

Daddy hugged him tight, but Harry screamed. Both his legs were broken. They rushed him to a hospital, where he stayed several weeks.

What a brave boy! For forty-five minutes he was down that well, with two broken legs, never giving up hope, never losing his head, and doing exactly what his daddy told him!

"He always did mind well," said his daddy proudly—and that's the real reason why Harry got out of that dreadful place alive.

STORY **29**

Georgia and
the Glass Bird

ONE FINE SUNDAY afternoon Georgia, her brother Geoffrey, and their cousin Ronnie, were standing on a street corner chatting, when one of them said, "Let's go for a walk."

"Where to?" asked Ronnie.

"Oh, I don't know," said Georgia. "It might be nice to go as far as Keene's flower shop. I always like to look at the fountain. I hope it's working today."

"Good idea," said Geoffrey. "Let's go."

So they sauntered down the street together until they came to the flower shop. Happily, the fountain was working, and the three children stood watching it.

It was a pretty scene, with water cascading into a pool full of lilies, dotted here and there with glass birds. It was like a lovely little bit of country that somebody had brought into town.

"How cold the water is!" said Georgia, stretching out her hand to the fountain.

"Look out for that bird!" cried Geoffrey.

The warning came too late.   149

As Georgia drew back her hand she touched one of the birds and its head broke off.

"You'll be in trouble now!" cried Geoffrey, running off at top speed, with Ronnie following close behind.

Georgia didn't run. She just stood there looking sadly at the broken bird, wondering what she should do. She thought she should tell the storekeeper but, because it was Sunday, the store was closed. There was nothing she could do but go home.

The boys were waiting for her—at a safe distance. They were full of advice, not very comforting.

"I wouldn't tell him," said Geoffrey.

"Neither would I," said Ronnie. "That Mr. Keene is mean. I bet he'd charge you ten dollars for that bird if he ever found out you broke it."

"You can be lucky it's Sunday and nobody was there," said Geoffrey.

"Don't worry," said Georgia, "I'll go back the very first thing tomorrow morning and offer to pay for it. I broke it,

and I should pay for it. I know I don't have enough money in my savings box, but maybe he will let me earn the rest."

As she mentioned her savings box her heart sank. She had been saving up for a long time and had three dollars and twenty-five cents in it. What if Mr. Keene should charge ten dollars for that bird, as Ronnie had said? That would be dreadful!

When they arrived home Georgia told Mother all that had happened, Geoffrey and Ronnie adding their comments now and then.

Mother looked thoughtful.

"Georgia says she's going to go back and tell Mr. Keene and pay for the ornament out of her savings," said Geoffrey. "Isn't she silly?"

"No," said Mother, "she isn't. I think she's right. We should always offer to pay for damage we cause, even if it is accidental."

Then turning to Georgia, she said, "By all means go and see Mr. Keene. Tell him just how it happened and that you

are willing to pay for the broken bird. I think he will appreciate it. We never lose by being honest."

Mother was right. Next morning Georgia went back to the flower shop. Half an hour later she returned with a beautiful bouquet in her hands, her face radiant with joy.

"Oh, Mother, it was wonderful!" she cried. "At first he looked very solemn and said he would have to charge me a lot of money. Then I saw a twinkle in his eye, and he said that, on second thought, the bill would be one quarter! So I gave it to him. Then what do you suppose! He gave me this lovely bunch of flowers. And when I was leaving he said I was the most honest little girl he'd ever met! Wasn't that nice of him?"

"It surely was, darling," said Mother, with tears in her eyes. "And so very, very true!"

30

Almost Home

JERRY WAS BORN on a farm in one of the Midwestern States of North America. As a boy he learned to ride a horse and roamed all over the wide-open spaces he could see from his home.

He loved everything about the place: the horses, the cows, the sheep, the dogs, the chickens; he loved the rambling old farmhouse and the room that he called his own; but most of all he loved his father and mother. Gladly he worked for them, in the house or in the fields.

As he grew up he hoped he would never have to leave the place. But one day he was called into the Army and sent off to fight in a foreign land.

But while his body was overseas, his heart was still at home. How he longed for the dreadful war to cease when he could return to the homeland and see his father and mother again! He often looked up at the stars when he was standing watch and dreamed of that happy time.

At last the day came, and he set off for home. After a long, long journey he arrived at the village where he was to catch the bus that went by his farm. Alas, when he got   153

to the bus station he found the last bus had gone.

Poor Jerry! What could he do now?

Stores and gas stations were all shut. To make things worse, it began to rain in torrents.

Suddenly, outside a garage, he spied a car marked "For Sale." It was a wreck of a car, with its windshield broken and one of its fenders off. But he thought to himself, If I can wake the man up, I'll buy it and drive home.

So he hammered on the door until somebody came. Then he bought the old car with the last money in his pocket and started for home in the middle of the night.

What did he care that it was raining hard?

What did he care that he was soaked to the skin?

He was going home! Every turn of the wheels, every bump of the road, cried, "Home, home, home!"

When at last he got there and saw his dear ones again, his joy was too great for words.

We, too, are on our way to our heavenly home. Every boy and girl who loves God is going there. It is a home full of beauty, light, and gladness. It has "many mansions"—

enough for everybody who wants to be there. And within its walls there is neither pain, nor sickness, nor death, nor tears. All the conflicts of this world will be forgotten.

We must let nothing hinder us from going there—neither trouble, nor hardship, nor suffering.

Through storm and darkness, rain and hail, we must go on toward our goal.

This glorious home is not far away. Every morning finds us closer to it. Every evening we are a day's march nearer to it. And everything that is happening in the world today, everything we do to tell people of Jesus and His love, cries, "Home, home, home!"

Someday soon we shall be there, and Jesus will meet us with open arms and a loving welcome. What a homecoming that will be!

The Ungrateful Nine

ON ONE OCCASION when Jesus was going into a village in Galilee, ten lepers called out to Him together, asking Him to heal them of their terrible disease.

"Jesus, Master, have mercy on us!" they cried (Luke 17:13, R.S.V.).

Jesus called back to them. "Go and show yourselves to the priests" (verse 14, R.S.V.)—which meant that they were to ask the priest to give them permission to go back among their people again.

Obeying, but wondering what the Great Healer meant, the ten went on their way to the priest.

Suddenly one said to another, "I feel better already." "So do I," said the others in chorus.

Then they looked at their hands, and, lo, the sores and scars were gone! They were healed!

One of the ten, a Samaritan, overjoyed at what had
happened, ran back to where Jesus was standing, and falling at His feet, thanked Him with all his heart for what He had done.

What about the other nine? That is just what Jesus asked. They went on their way, happy enough, doubtless, that they had been healed, but forgetting all about the One who had healed them.

But think of it! They had been cured of the most dreadful of all diseases, and yet they did not even turn around to say, "Thank You."

Jesus was very much disappointed. Turning to His disciples, He said, "Were not ten cleansed? Where are the nine?" (verse 17, R.S.V.).

Some boys and girls who have kind things done for them are like that Samaritan who came back and said, "Thank You." But many of them, I am afraid, are like the nine who did not come back. Let us never disappoint Jesus by being ungrateful for the good things He gives us so freely. And sometimes, too, I believe Mother would be glad to hear a little "Thank you" for all she does for you every day.

32

Larry's Leopards

THIS STORY CAME to me from the mother of a 6-year-old boy. All I have changed is his name, in case he might be teased by his schoolmates about the prayer he made.

Little Larry had been looking forward eagerly to going to school. Mother had bought him a new outfit of clothes of which he was very proud. But on the very day school opened he fell sick, so sick that Mother sent for the doctor.

The doctor came and looked Larry over. Then he shook his head solemnly and said Larry must stay in bed.

Poor Larry! What a disappointment! All the other children were going to school while he stayed in bed!

Every morning when he woke up he hoped he would feel better, but he didn't. Instead he got weaker and weaker.

Mother spent all her time taking care of Larry. All day she watched over him with a terrible sadness in her heart, and all night she stayed on a cot by his side.

Sometimes, when Larry seemed a little brighter, she would read to him from *Uncle Arthur's Bedtime Stories,* especially the Bible stories, which Larry loved best of all.

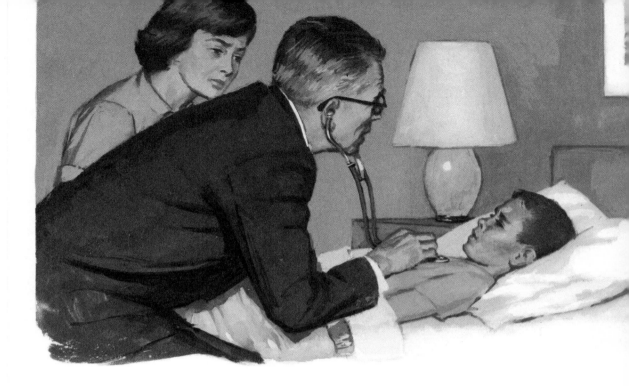

Often he would go off to sleep right in the middle of a story, but when he woke up he would say, "You didn't finish the story." And Mother would begin reading again just where she had left off.

The story he liked best was the one about the ten lepers whom Jesus healed, and the one who came back to thank Him. Just what went through little Larry's mind as he listened to this story, I don't know, but he loved it, and, ever more weakly as the days went by, he would ask Mother to read it again.

By this time Mother was becoming very worried. She didn't like the look on the doctor's face when he examined Larry. Gradually the awful truth dawned upon her that her precious little boy was not going to live much longer. She wired Daddy, who was away on a long trip, to come home at once.

That evening, when Mother was so worn out with sleepless nights and anxious grief that she couldn't look at Larry

without tears rolling down her cheeks, he opened his eyes and said, "Why are you crying, Mother?"

"Because you are so sick," she said, "and I don't like to see you sick."

"Then why don't you ask Jesus to make me better like He made the leopards?"

"The leopards?" asked Mother. "What leopards?"

"The leopards in the story, Mother," said Larry. "You know. There were ten of them, and one of them came walking back and said, 'Thank You, Jesus.' Remember?"

"Of course I remember, darling," said Mother, smiling. "The ten lepers, and 'The Ungrateful Nine.' And I should have remembered long ago to ask Jesus for help. I suppose I've been too busy and too tired."

"Is it too late to ask Him now?" whispered Larry.

"Oh, darling, no!" cried Mother. "It's never too late. We will ask Him right away. You and I together."

Folding Larry's hands and putting her own hands over

them, she began to pray. But Larry interrupted her.

"Please, Jesus," he said very faintly, "make me better like You did the leopards, and I'll thank You. I promise."

Then Mother prayed, too.

When Larry opened his eyes he looked up into Mother's face and said, "I'm feeling better, Mother."

Mother could hardly believe her ears, but there *was* a change in Larry. She could see it.

When the doctor called that evening a strange look came over his face as he looked at Larry. "Something has happened," he said. "I believe he is going to get well."

Next day, for the first time in weeks, Larry sat up. Two days later, when Daddy arrived, half expecting to attend a funeral, Larry was able to walk out to greet him.

Nobody could understand it. Neither Daddy nor the doctor nor the neighbors. Nobody, that is, except Mother and Larry—and Jesus.

Of course, He understood best of all. And what did it matter to Him whether Larry said leopards or lepers? Here was a little boy full of faith and love—and Jesus answered his simple prayer.

33

How Gary
Got Home
From School

THIS STORY CAME to me from south Wales, and I know you will enjoy it as much as I did when I first read Gary's letter.

One afternoon, when Gary was about ten years old, he went to the playing field with his friend Jonathan. After the game they both entered the dressing room to change.

Both were slow dressers, with Gary a bit slower than Jonathan.

"Better hurry up," said Jonathan on the way out, "or you'll miss the bus."

Gary began hurrying, but not fast enough. Pretty soon he was the only boy left in the dressing room.

Now he couldn't find his coat. He hunted all over for it in vain. Only Jonathan's coat was hanging on the rack.

Suddenly it dawned upon him that Jonathan had taken *his* coat by mistake, and the only thing for him to do was to wear his friend's coat.

This he did, but his season ticket for the bus was in the pocket of his own coat—and Jonathan was wearing it!

162 Now he really did hurry, running as fast as he could to

the bus stop, only to see the bus pulling away with Jonathan on board!

What to do next? He didn't know. Anxiously he felt in all his pockets—his own trousers pockets and Jonathan's coat pockets. All he could find was the return half of a bus ticket to Swansea and three pennies!

He decided to take the next bus to Swansea and then another bus home. It was a long way round—miles out of his way—but there seemed nothing else to do. So when the Swansea bus came along he jumped on board.

Arriving at last in Swansea, he found he didn't have enough money to pay for the bus ticket home.

Then he thought he would telephone his father, but he needed another penny to place the call. Where could he find one?

He searched everywhere, walking up and down the street to see if perchance somebody might have lost a penny, but nobody had. He could have asked a policeman for one, but he didn't. He was afraid the policeman might not understand why he wanted a penny so badly.

At this moment a bus came by that was going near his home. It stopped, and he asked the fare. It was far more than his three pennies, so he had to watch the bus drive away.

Now he really *was* in a fix. Twelve miles from home, and no means of getting there! Night was coming on, too.

In his letter he said, "It was then that I thought of *Bedtime Stories* and how children in difficulty have prayed to Jesus to help them, and I wondered whether He would help me too. So I closed my eyes and said, 'Please, Jesus, send some sort of help to get me home.' "

You'll never guess what happened next.

When he opened his eyes he walked slowly over to the nearest bus stop, for no particular reason. Several people were standing in line waiting for the next bus.

Suddenly someone called out, "Hello, Gary. What in the world are you doing here?"

It was his next-door neighbor! Happily, somebody who knew him was at his side!

"Am I glad to see you!" cried Gary, pouring out his troubles.

Of course the neighbor gladly paid his fare, and tired but happy, Gary arrived home about 10:00 P.M.

Several years have passed since then, but Gary's heart is still filled with gratitude to the One who sent him help in his hour of need. Never will he forget how the dear Lord Jesus heard and answered his prayer.

34

Sandy Disappears

SANDY, I SHOULD EXPLAIN, is not a boy or a girl, but a ratlike creature with large cheek pouches. She is a hamster and belongs to a little girl called Jill.

For myself, I must confess, I don't really care for rats, even when they do have big cheek pouches, any more than I like mice, whether they be white or brown. But there's no accounting for taste, as the old saying goes, and some children think these creatures are perfectly lovely.

As for 8-year-old Jill, she loved Sandy better than her best doll, and sometimes, one would think, more than her Mother, Daddy, Baby Brother, and the rest of the family put together.

Sandy was the pride of her life, the joy of her heart, the apple of her eye. She talked more about Sandy's funny little antics than she did about anything else.

One of her school friends said she was "nuts" about the "rat," but that didn't upset her. The more she was teased about her pet the more she loved it.

She wanted to put Sandy's cage in the living room, but Mother drew the line at that. She didn't like the smell for one thing, and for another, she was afraid the animal might get out.

So Jill had to keep Sandy in the back bedroom where there was no furniture and no carpet on the floor.

And it was there that Sandy disappeared.

One day as Jill took her pet out of the cage to stroke her, Sandy suddenly broke loose, scurried down her dress, and scampered across the floor.

How Sandy knew there was a hole in those floor boards, I don't know. Neither does Jill, nor anybody else, for that matter. But straight for the hole went Sandy, and in less time than it takes to tell she was out of sight.

"Come back! Come back!" cried Jill, but she might just as well have saved her breath. Sandy didn't take the slightest notice.

Jill was crushed. It was as though all the lights had gone out in her little world.

"Daddy!" she cried. "Mother! Sandy's gone!"

Daddy came hurrying.

"Whatever's the matter?" he asked.

"Sandy has disappeared," she wailed. "I took her out of

her cage to love her, and she ran away and went down that hole in the floor boards."

"Where else did you expect her to go?" asked Daddy. "It's the most natural thing in the world for rats and mice to go down holes. That's the way they live when little girls don't put them in cages."

"But I want my Sandy back," cried Jill.

"I wouldn't worry too much," said Daddy. "She's probably having the time of her life running around in the dark all through the house. Maybe she's down in the basement by now looking for a way out."

"Then she'll never come back!" cried Jill. "Oh, my poor Sandy! Isn't there anything I can do to make her come back?"

"You could try putting some food in the cage and leaving the cage door open by the hole. If she can't find food anywhere else she might possibly come back here."

"Would it help if I were to pray for her?" asked Jill.

"It might," said Daddy. "You never can tell."

"Well, I am going to," said Jill. "I love Sandy, and I want her back ever so badly."

So she prayed. That night and all the next day. She also did what Daddy had suggested—put food in the cage, leaving it open beside the hole in the floor. Every little while she would look in the room, hoping against hope that Sandy might have come back. But she didn't come.

Maybe you think she shouldn't have prayed about such a lowly creature as a hamster. But why not? It isn't the kind of thing we pray for that matters, or its size or shape. It's the love in the heart of the one who prays.

More than anything else in all the world God loves little girls and boys. He loves to hear them talk to Him. He loves to surprise them when they ask Him for help. Said Jesus, "Let the children come to me, do not hinder them; for to such belongs the kingdom of God" (Mark 10:14, R.S.V.).

Maybe when God saw pure love in Jill's heart and heard her plaintive cry for help He sent Sandy back. Don't ask me how. I don't know. But one morning when Jill went into that back bedroom Sandy was in her cage, just as though she had never been away.

"I was so glad, I cried," Jill says in her letter. "I thanked God with all my heart. And I shall remember that day until I die."

I am sure she will. And when she is grown up and has children of her own—and they have hamsters and white mice and dogs and cats and rabbits and things—she will teach her boys and girls to take their troubles to God, and all heaven and earth will be the happier.

35

Steve and the Steamboat

STEVE LIVED NEAR a very wide river, big enough for steamboats to sail on. It was long ago.

One day he went down to the riverbank where there was a small and rather rickety old pier. As he walked to the end of the pier he pulled a handkerchief out of his pocket and began to wave it.

"What do you think you're waving at?" asked a man who was fishing from the pier.

"Nothing," said Steve. "But the steamer is due here in a few minutes, and I was just getting ready for it."

"The steamer doesn't stop here," said the man. "If you want to catch it, you'd better go to the next pier two miles down."

"But it's going to stop here today," said Steve.

"It isn't," said the man. "It never does. You're just making a big mistake."

"I'm not," said Steve. "It really is going to stop here."

"It isn't," said the man. "You're just a foolish little boy. Why don't you take advice from someone who knows?"

Just then they both caught sight of a billow of smoke 169

170 rising beyond a bend in the river.

"She's coming!" cried Steve.

"You'd better start running," said the man, "or you'll never get to the next pier in time."

"I don't need to run," said Steve. "It's going to stop here."

"It isn't," said the man angrily. "You ought to know better."

Now the big old steamboat was in full view, coming toward them at top speed, its great paddle wheels churning up the water into froth and foam.

Steve began to wave frantically.

"Can't you see it's not going to stop here?" said the man. "It's going too fast."

"But it is going to stop," said Steve as his handkerchief fluttered to and fro.

All of a sudden the steamboat began to slow down. The paddle wheels were not turning so rapidly. Then they stopped altogether and began to go the other way as the steamer glided more and more slowly toward the rickety old pier.

Very gently it came to a stop, and a gangplank was lowered.

Steve walked up it, stuffing his handkerchief into his pocket as he went. Then he turned and looked at the man on the pier.

"You see, it did stop," he said.

"I don't know why," said the man grumpily.

"Oh, that's easy," said Steve. "You see, the captain is my daddy!"

What a sweet and lovely thought!—especially when you think of God and His care for us all.

Some people think He is too big to be bothered with little boys and girls and too busy to listen to their prayers.

But it isn't true. He *is* interested. He *does* care. He is our loving Father and is concerned about all that happens to us.

As the Bible says, "As a father pities his children so the Lord pities those who fear him" (Psalm 103:13, R.S.V.).

No matter who you are, or how little you are, or where you live, if you tell God that you need Him (just like Steve waved his hanky to his daddy for help), He will help you.

How Does God Speak?

ROSEMARY, TED, and their friend Jack were playing ball on the back lawn. Suddenly they heard a bell tinkle.

"What's that?" asked Jack, who lived on the opposite side of town.

"Oh, that's the worship bell," said Rosemary.

"The what?" asked Jack.

"The worship bell," repeated Rosemary. "Mother rings it every evening about this time. Then we all go in for family worship."

"You mean you have to stop playing just for that?"

"Why, yes, of course," smiled Rosemary. "We love it. We sing hymns together. Then Mother—or Daddy, when he's home—reads a story from the Bible. After that we ask questions about it, and then one of us says a little prayer. You'd enjoy it. Why don't you join us tonight?"

"Sounds pretty dull to me," said Jack. "But I'll come with you once just to see what it's like."

As they walked up the garden path they could hear Mother playing a hymn on the piano, but she stopped to

173

◀ Painting by William Hutchinson © Review and Herald

Steve turned as he walked up the gangplank and said, "You see, the captain is my daddy."

give Jack a special welcome and make him feel at home.
Then they all sang hymns together for the next ten minutes.

For a Bible story Mother chose the one about Samuel, the little boy who lived in the temple with Eli, the high priest. Samuel's mother wanted him to serve in God's temple, hoping that some day he would become a great man for God. So she made him a little garment, just like the priests wore. Little Samuel loved being with Eli and helped him by doing little jobs around the temple.

One night, you remember, he heard a voice calling "Samuel, Samuel," and he thought Eli wanted him. But Eli hadn't said a word. After this had happened twice, Eli told him what to say should he hear the voice again.

Later that same night Samuel did hear it again, and this time he said, "Speak, for thy servant hears" (1 Samuel 3:10, R.S.V.). God answered and talked with him for quite a while.

As Mother closed the Bible she said, "Now it's question time. Who wants to be first?"

"I do," said Jack, holding up his hand as if he were in school.

"That's fine," said Mother. "What would you like to ask?"

"If God spoke to that boy Samuel," said Jack, "why hasn't He spoken to me?"

"Maybe He has," said Mother.

"I never heard Him," said Jack.

"Are you sure?" asked Mother. "It could be you weren't listening."

"Does God always speak out loud?" asked Ted.

"Oh, no," said Mother. "Most times, I think, He speaks very softly, softer than a whisper."

"I think God spoke to me the other day," said Rosemary.

"Tell us about it," said Mother.

◀ Painting by Russell Harlan © by Review and Herald

The call of God to the boy Samuel in the temple and how he became a great prophet is popular in every story circle.

"Well, I was going to stay after school and play with the girls a little while when a voice seemed to say to me, 'Go home at once; your Mother may need you.' So I ran home and found you with that bad headache."

"I remember, darling, and I was so glad to see you. I had been praying that you would come soon so you could run to the drugstore for me."

"Do you think God spoke to me then?" asked Rosemary.

"I'm sure He did," said Mother. "And now let me tell you something that happened to me. Last week I was deeply impressed to go to the hospital to visit a friend. So I dropped my work right in the middle of the morning and went to see her. When I got there she said to me, 'I prayed all night that you would come this morning.' Wasn't that wonderful? I'm sure God passed on her message to me."

"Do you think God might speak to me someday?" asked Jack.

"Of course," said Mother. "But remember, He speaks in all sorts of ways and in all sorts of places, so you'll have to keep listening. By the way, don't you have a new baby sister?"

"Yes," said Jack.

"Then your mother must be very busy. Probably she isn't getting much sleep and is very tired. It could be, Jack, that God is trying to get through to you with the message, 'Please help Mother with the dishes,' or 'Don't forget to wash the kitchen floor for her,' or 'Mind the baby for her now and then.' "

"Do you think God says things like that?" asked Jack.

"I'm sure He does," said Mother. "But, of course, if you should happen to be too busy seeking a good time for yourself, it's possible you might not hear Him."

Jack smiled. He had gotten the point.

"Now let's say our evening prayer," said Mother. Then they all knelt, and Mother asked God to help each one to

walk so close to Him from day to day that none would ever
fail to hear His call.

When they arose from their knees, Jack said good-by
and started off home. There was a new light in his eye and a
new look on his face. He was listening for the voice of God.
Indeed, he felt sure he had heard it already.

37

The Forbidden Ride

COLIN WAS SUCH a good little boy that Daddy gave him a bicycle on his 6th birthday. He was so happy that he rode it all day long.

Strangely, he didn't seem to be so good after that. Mother began to have a lot of trouble with him because he *would* ride the bicycle when she wanted him to help her. Then, too, he started showing off to his friends by riding with bare feet and keeping his hands off the handle bars.

Mother wondered whether giving him the bicycle had been such a good idea after all. Maybe Daddy had given it to him too soon. But it was too late to take it away now, especially since Colin rode it to school and back. Perhaps if she talked to him it would help.

"Colin," she said, as he came in from school one afternoon, "I want to talk to you about your bicycle."

"What about it?"

"Well," said Mother, "I'm glad you are so happy with it, but I wish you wouldn't show off so much. Riding without your hands on the handle bars may look smart, but it's very dangerous, especially for a boy of your age, and with so much traffic on the roads."

"Pshaw!" said Colin, "there's nothing to it. All the kids do it, and nobody gets hurt."

"Maybe not yet," said Mother, "but somebody will. And there's that other foolish thing you do—riding with bare feet."

"What's the matter with that?" asked Colin, as if he were twice his age.

"Just this," said Mother. "One day you will get a foot caught in the spokes, or maybe a toe caught in the chain, and that could hurt a lot."

"Ha, ha, ha!" laughed Colin. "Just as though I would ever do anything like that."

"Bigger boys than you have done it," said Mother.

"But I'll never do anything so stupid," said Colin.

"I hope you don't," said Mother. "And to make sure, I forbid you to ride again with bare feet. What's more, apart from going to school, I don't want you to ride anywhere without telling me first. Understand?"

"You mean I have to ask you every time I go for a ride?" asked Colin.

"Every time you leave this house," said Mother. "Then I shall know where you are and that you have your shoes on."

"Oh," cried Colin, pouting, "what a life!"

"It's all for your good, dear, as you'll find out someday. And when you are a little older, things can be different."

Colin scowled and went off to play with his bicycle—be-

ing careful to ride only on the path around the house.

Then he began to say to himself, "I don't see why I can't ride with bare feet. Other boys do it. And if Mother were a boy my age she'd ride with bare feet too. I'm not going to tell her every time I ride away from the house. That's too much. There's no reason why I should do it at all."

It's dangerous to think thoughts like these, for they always lead to trouble. Indeed, within half an hour Colin was riding out of the gate—with bare feet.

But he was soon back, his mother told me, crying his heart out and leaving a trail of blood behind him as he limped toward the house.

"What happened?" she asked as she ran toward him and picked him up. "What have you done? I thought you were playing by yourself in the garden."

Amid his tears and cries of pain Colin explained.

He had sneaked out for a ride, hoping Mother would never find out. Then he had

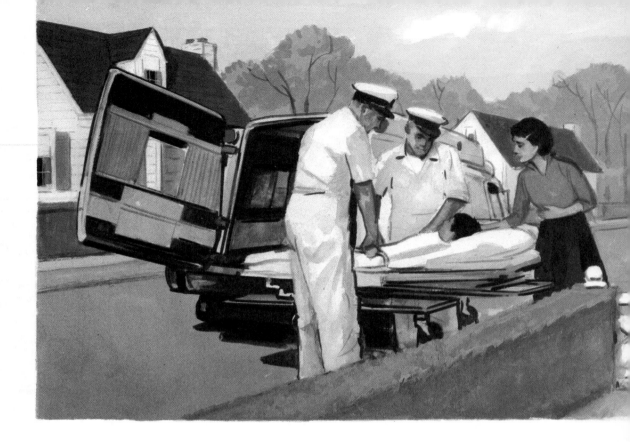

begun riding with only one hand on the handle bars. The bike had hit a bump in the road and wobbled badly. His foot had slipped off the pedal and had caught between the chain and the big cogwheel.

"Ouch!" he cried as Mother tried to clean the wound. "Is it cut badly?" he asked.

"Very badly," Mother said. "We'd better get you to the hospital right away or you may lose your big toe."

Colin groaned while a neighbor telephoned for an ambulance.

"Oh, why did I do it?" he cried.

"That's what Adam must have said when he left the Garden of Eden," said Mother. "There's an awful price to pay for disobedience."

This time it was part of a big toe.

38

Under the Pier

ALL WEEK LONG Charlie had been coaxing Mother to take him to the seaside. "Just for one little day, Mother," he had said.

"Sorry," Mother had replied, "I can't possibly go this week. I've got far too much to do. I'll take you next week. Next Sunday, for sure."

"For sure?" Charlie had asked.

"For sure," Mother had said.

So Charlie waited another week. But now, with Mother's promise so definite, he got everything ready to go. His bucket and shovel. His little sailing boat. His beach ball. His swim suit. His sandals. Such a lot of things!

He put them all in a pile and kept adding to it as he thought of other things to take along.

At last Sunday came.

Bright and early Charlie was out of bed. He ran to the window and looked out.

It was raining! His heart sank.

"What are we going to do?" he wailed as he met Mother in the kitchen. "It *would* have to rain on the only day we can possibly go!"

"Why bother about a little rain?" said Mother.

"You mean we're going?"

"Of course we're going," said Mother. "I am sure it will clear up later, and we'll sit under the pier until it does."

Overjoyed, Charlie threw all his precious things into the car, and they started off.

It certainly wasn't the best sort of day for a trip to the seaside. The sky was dull gray, and everything was dripping wet.

Mother parked her car as near to the pier as she could. Then she and Charlie hurried to take shelter under it as fast as they could go. Mother carried the lunch baskets and Charlie, his bucket, shovel, sailing boat, beach ball, swim suit, and all the rest.

Under the pier they found a stretch of dry sand, and

Mother made herself comfortable. Charlie put on his swim suit, then took his sailing boat down to the water, which was very calm that morning, probably because of the rain.

By and by he came back to mother and began to dig a big hole in the sand.

Pretty soon Mother said it was time to eat and opened up the two lunch baskets. She had prepared all sorts of delicious foods as an extraspecial treat for Charlie, and he shouted in delight as he looked them over.

While they ate they became aware of two elderly ladies sitting in deck chairs not far away, blankets wrapped tightly around them. They were grumbling to each other in loud voices.

"Wretched day!" said one.

"Miserable day!" said the other.

"Always rains in this place," said the first lady. "I don't know why I ever came here."

"Nor do I," said the other. "Horrible place! So cold and wet. Sorry we came."

"Why are they grumbling so?" Charlie asked Mother.

"I don't know," said Mother. "Must have got out of bed on the wrong side this morning, I should say."

By and by the two ladies got out of their chairs and came over to Mother and Charlie.

"We've been watching you two," they said, "and we can't make out why you can both be so cheerful on such a miserable day as this."

"Well," said Mother, smiling, "we made up our minds we would be happy even though it is raining. And we're having a great time, aren't we, Charlie?"

"I should say we are!" said Charlie.

Then, just like a boy, he added, "Why don't you two come over and join us? Then you'd be happy too."

The glum look on the two faces disappeared. Both old ladies actually smiled.

"May we?" they asked.

"Of course you may," said Mother.

So they dragged their deck chairs over to where Mother and Charlie were sitting, and Mother offered them some of her lunch.

Soon they were all chatting away, happy as could be.

Just then the sun came out.

"Well, did you ever!" said one of the old ladies. "Look, the sun is shining!"

"So it is!" said Mother. But it didn't mean quite so much to her and Charlie, for it had been shining in their hearts all the time.

Complete Index

Lesson
Index

189